Hitler's *Mein Kampf* in Britain and America
A Publishing History 1930–39

Hitler's *Mein Kampf* in Britain and America

A Publishing History 1930–39

James J. Barnes and Patience P. Barnes

Cambridge University Press

Cambridge

London   New York   New Rochelle
Melbourne   Sydney

CAMBRIDGE UNIVERSITY PRESS
Cambridge, New York, Melbourne, Madrid, Cape Town, Singapore, São Paulo

Cambridge University Press
The Edinburgh Building, Cambridge CB2 8RU, UK

Published in the United States of America by Cambridge University Press, New York

www.cambridge.org
Information on this title: www.cambridge.org/9780521226912

First published 1980
This digitally printed version 2008

A catalogue record for this publication is available from the British Library

ISBN 978-0-521-22691-2 hardback
ISBN 978-0-521-07267-0 paperback

To Bertha, Harry, Elinor, and Charles

Contents

Preface

Somewhere we read that Hitler's *Mein Kampf* was not available in an English translation until 1939. That piqued our curiosity, and we began to investigate the reasons for the delay. It turned out that an abridgment appeared in 1933, yet why only an abridgment? The mystery grew as we asked other questions, and some of the answers were only known, it appeared, to certain people who were actually involved in the early attempts to publish *Mein Kampf*. Many people who might have been helpful with our inquiry are now dead, but it surprised us to find quite a number who are still living. The following story is the result of five years of investigation, often spent in fascinating conversation or meticulous correspondence, endeavouring to tidy up details with members of the inter-war generation who recalled the circumstances.

The Acknowledgments will hopefully convey some notion of our deep gratitude to those who helped us in this undertaking. We would like to single out one person here for special attention. Irmingard McKinney worked with us on the procurement and translation of German-language documents, and without her assistance we would not have felt in a position to embark upon the project.

J.J.B. & P.P.B.

Crawfordsville, Indiana

Acknowledgments

C. C. Aronsfeld for gladly sharing his knowledge about the different translations of *Mein Kampf*; The Duke of Atholl for making available materials at Blair Castle relating to the Duchess of Atholl; Auswärtiges Amt, Bonn, for cordial assistance on all occasions; Mr and Mrs John Baird, for helping to make some important contacts; R. E. Barker of the Publishers' Association, for encouragement and help; Berlin Document Centre, for extremely thorough assistance in locating materials; Roberta Berry, for excellent typing; Board of Deputies of British Jews, London; E. K. Bramsted; Neville Brown, for suggestions and encouragement; Susan Buck-Morss, for help with examining materials; Bundesarchiv, Koblenz; Jonathan Bush, for help with reading and research; Pierce Butler; Prof. Elias Clark, for kind permission to quote from the C. E. Clark papers; Ian Colvin; Curtis Brown Ltd; Prof. Richard Danzig; Norris Darrell, for kind permission to quote from the Learned Hand papers; Prof. Sander Diamond; D. N. Dilks, for helpful observations and permission to quote; Nancy Doemel, for help with research; Seth Dubin, for vital help and encouragement early in the project; James Ducker, for diligently locating and clarifying various research queries; Mrs G. M. Dugdale for her cordial hospitality and assistance; Sir William Dugdale for his kind cooperation and information; H. I. Feingold; Lady Fergusson of Kilkerran (daughter of E. T. S. Dugdale); Foreign and Commonwealth Office Library, for greatly

Acknowledgments

facilitating the examination of material in their possession; Roger Fulford; Mr and Mrs Joseph Gawrys, for extraordinary help with one phase of the research; Sue Glennon, for help with reading and research; Elaine Greenlee, for help with reading and research; Prof. Gerald Gunther, for great help with locating items among the Learned Hand papers; Prof. O. J. Hale; Geoffrey Halliday for valuable responses to all our queries; Harcourt Brace Jovanovich, and especially Rita Vaughan, for making our examination of the Reynal & Hitchcock papers so convenient and expeditious; Harvard Law School Library, for facilitating the use of the Learned Hand papers; Mrs Curtice Hitchcock, for cordial response to our inquiries; Hoover Institution on War, Revolution, and Peace, for unfailing courtesy and help with our many requests; Houghton Library of Harvard University; Houghton Mifflin Co., for cordial cooperation over many years; Hutchinson Publishing Group Ltd; D. G. Hutton, for most valuable responses to all our queries; Institute of Contemporary History and the Wiener Library, London: we are most grateful not only for opportunities to examine material in the Wiener Library and to consult the Library's staff, but also for permission to reprint as Chapter 1 in this volume our article which first appeared in Volume XXVII (1974) of the *Wiener Library Bulletin*; Mary Johnson for very good reading of the typescript; Cherry Kearton for his most kind cooperation at the outset of this undertaking; Prof. G. O. Kent; Frau Dr Greta Kuckoff for responding to all our questions with valuable insights; Prof. W. L. Langer; Larry LeSeure, for a preliminary look at the Clark papers; K. W. Lore, for prompt cooperation; Sir Robert Lusty; Ralph Manheim, for valuable clarifications relating to his 1943 translation of *Mein Kampf*; Irene Mitchell for help with reading and research; Constance Moore, for good help with reading and research; Lilian T. Mowrer; Mrs James Murphy, for her indispensable help and

Acknowledgments

unfailing cooperation; J. Barrows Mussey, for his hearty and extensive cooperation; National Archives, Washington, and especially Robert Wolfe and John Mendelsohn, for calling to our attention those microfilms that were most pertinent to our project; National Register of Archives (Scotland), for extraordinary kindness in fetching and photocopying materials; Tam Neville, for considerable help with reading and research; Patricia Radinger, for help with reading and research; Register of Copyrights Office, Library of Congress, for valuable assistance with our inquiries about James Murphy; Mrs Virginia Reis, for considerable help and information; Mrs Eugène Reynal, for valuable suggestions; A. V. Savage for kind permission to quote from the Memoranda of A. N. Hand; W. N. Seymour, for help in securing information about the C. E. Clark papers; G. N. Shuster, for his long and thoughtful responses to our questions; Prof. Michael Smith, for valuable help in locating items among the Clark papers; D. H. Soskin, for helpful cooperation throughout; Mrs Leonard Stein, for welcome background information; George Stewart, for background information on the Stackpole firm; Martha Taylor, for completing the typing with such efficiency and accommodation; United States Department of Justice, Civil Division, for information about royalty payments as stipulated by the Trading with the Enemy Act; Wabash College, for several most timely research grants; Wabash College Library, for the unfailing and cheerful cooperation of its Librarian and staff; Prof. D. C. Watt, for important suggestions; Sir J. W. Wheeler-Bennett; William Wieland, for continued and valuable help with German-language materials; Philip Wittenberg, for essential information on key issues; Prof. William Woehrlin, for encouragement and assistance in the early stages of this project; Yale Law School Library, for ready access to the C. E. Clark papers; Yivo Institute, New York; Virginia Zachary, for much help with our voluminous correspondence.

I

Mein Kampf in Britain, 1930–39

Had Hitler not gone to prison in 1924, he might never have written his autobiography, *Mein Kampf*. Captured soon after an unsuccessful *putsch* in Munich, he was duly tried, found guilty, and sent to Landsberg prison where he was confined in comparatively spacious and comfortable quarters and given full access to visitors, books, and newspapers. Several of his close Party associates, including Rudolf Hess, were there to assist him. During this enforced leisure, it is not surprising that he began to write his memoirs.

These were not to be the ordinary reminiscences of a defeated and discredited politician, however. Hitler needed to build a legend, not only about himself, but about the Nazi movement. He had to show the world how he had struggled as a youth against adversity, how he had come through the war creditably, and how he had gradually come to be the leader of a new party. The Party had met with reverses because of the treachery of some whose malefactions would be exposed in the book he was to write. In *Mein Kampf* he would set forth the future directions of a potentially great movement with an appeal to all Germans, and a defiant warning to Germany's enemies.

The first volume of Hitler's autobiography, *Mein Kampf*, was published in Germany in 1925, the second in 1926. It was a relatively expensive work selling for 24 Reichsmarks, but as later editions came out its price dropped. A one-volume edition published in 1930 sold for 8 Reichsmarks, and still

1

cheaper versions were issued in 1932 and 1933. Hitler's becoming Chancellor on 30 January 1933 naturally gave a great boost to sales, and by the autumn of that year the official Nazi publishing house in Munich, Eher Verlag, boasted that it had printed a million copies.[1]

That same autumn saw the first translations abroad. A one-volume English-language abridgment appeared in London under the imprint of Hurst & Blackett, a subsidiary of the Hutchinson Publishing Group Ltd. The same abridgment, with slightly different preliminary matter, was published by Houghton Mifflin Co. in Boston and New York.[2] In England Hitler's title was rendered *My Struggle*, while in America it was called *My Battle*. Another difference was that the London edition did not specify the translator's name whereas Americans were informed that it was E. T. S. Dugdale. About a dozen other translations appeared in various countries during the 1930s, but it was not until early 1939 that the full text was made available by Hurst & Blackett and Houghton Mifflin. By this time Austria had been incorporated into the Third Reich and Czechoslovakia had been desperately compromised by the Munich agreement. People began to have the uncomfortable feeling that *Mein Kampf* might be a blueprint for future aggression and that therefore the full text should be available.

A good deal of ambiguity surrounds the Dugdale edition. Why wasn't the complete work issued in 1933? Was it true, as some alleged, that Hitler refused to authorize the full text for fear of offending foreigners or revealing too many of his ultimate plans? Was the 1933 edition so expurgated as to be positively misleading, or did it convey adequately the essence of Hitler's doctrine? Why did publishers wait so long to make even an abridgment available to the public?

The ravages of the Second World War have greatly complicated the task of answering these questions, as virtually all the business records of Eher Verlag and of Hurst & Blackett were destroyed. In addition, several key individuals such as Walter Hutchinson the publisher, and Edgar Trevelyan Stratford Dugdale the translator, are no longer living. However, others with keen memories and cordial dispositions have patiently assisted us with the process of reconstruction.[3]

Contrary to earlier impressions, Hitler's publisher very much wanted to promote an English-language translation of his autobiography. In 1925 and 1927 appropriate steps were taken to register the title of *Mein Kampf* in America for purposes of copyright protection, and in 1928 the translation rights were offered to a British firm. Negotiations in both countries were assigned to a prominent literary agency, Curtis Brown Ltd, with offices in London, New York and Berlin. At this time few people in Germany, let alone abroad, were paying much attention to Hitler. *Mein Kampf* was therefore merely one of a number of books, and an obscure one at that, which Cherry Kearton, a Curtis Brown employee, picked up in Germany in 1928 on his way back to London after a European holiday. Once back on the job, Kearton tried to interest publisher after publisher in the book, but because it was a long, tedious work of 782 pages which made exceedingly dreary reading, no one would buy it. Not until September 1930 when the Nazis were rocketed from ninth to second largest party in the Reichstag did Hitler's name draw attention outside Germany, and by this time the Great Depression was making publishers more cautious about speculating in translations. Thus in 1931, when Geoffrey Halliday became Kearton's assistant at Curtis Brown, the two volumes of *Mein Kampf* were well out of sight, more or less forgotten in the storeroom.

Meanwhile, inspired by the same Reichstag elections, a completely separate effort for a translation was taking place. While travelling on the Continent, Mrs Blanche E. C. Dugdale was quick to recognize in the situation an opportunity for her husband to translate *Mein Kampf*. She knew he was well

3

qualified, as he was virtually bilingual and was already compiling a four-volume abridgment of German diplomatic documents based on the massive *Die Grosse Politik*. She wrote to him:[4]

apropos of work – I have an idea, but I dare say you feel too busy with your other book to consider it – however here it is for whatever it is worth. I gather, from references in the foreign papers I have read this week, that Hitler has written some kind of Autobiography. I am certain that *if* that has not been translated already, a publisher would consider it just now . . . But I know nothing more about the matter than that. Either the R.I.I.A. [Royal Institute of International Affairs] Library – or Hugh Latimer (Jack W.B.'s man, whom you know) might know the book – or where you could get a look at it. Then it would be possible to discover whether any translation has been made – or is being made. If you thought of taking the matter up I suppose you would offer it to Methuen – otherwise I would suggest Gollancz as the sort of publisher. Leonard Stein has just become a partner there – is much on the look-out for topical books – also Gollancz publishes a good deal for the Jewish market – and while all the world is interested in Hitler just now the Jews are specially and painfully so – on account of the Anti-Semitism which is part of the Nat. Socialist programme.

However – as I say – I suspect you feel you have not time just now.

It was natural for Blanche Dugdale to take a lively interest in international affairs. She was the niece of the former Prime Minister, Arthur James Balfour, and ardently shared his enthusiasm for establishing a Zionist state. Throughout the 1920s she was active in the League of Nations Union, served as a British delegate to the League in 1932, and frequently lectured at home and abroad on Zionism. In connection with the latter she got to know Leonard Stein who was Chairman of the Information Committee of the Board of Deputies of British Jews and of the Anglo-Jewish Association.

Edgar Dugdale also took an active interest in European affairs. After attending Eton and Balliol College, Oxford, he spent several years on the Continent learning foreign languages in the hope of becoming a British Foreign Service officer. Upon his return he married Blanche, familiarly known as Baffy, and took up residence in London. During the First World War he served with the Leicestershire Yeomanry, rose to the rank of captain, became ill in the trenches, and completed his wartime assignment in the Postal Censorship Service. His main occupation after the war was writing and translating, enhanced by his contacts at the Foreign Office and within the journalistic fraternity.[5] It is not exactly clear when he decided to translate *Mein Kampf*, but it was probably sometime in 1931 after finishing work on the German diplomatic documents. Friends testify that he had trouble finding anyone to publish it, just as Kearton had already discovered. He quietly abandoned it and turned his attention to other matters.

The London morning newspapers of 31 January 1933 broke the news of Hitler's Chancellorship. Cherry Kearton was not slow to act. His transfer the previous year from the Curtis Brown literary agency to the publishing firm of Hurst & Blackett had shifted his perspective toward acquiring, not disposing of, literary rights. He telephoned Geoffrey Halliday who was still at Curtis Brown to ask whether the copy of *Mein Kampf* was still there and whether Hurst & Blackett could purchase the translation rights. The copy was retrieved, but the quoted asking price was an almost unbelievable £350! This made Kearton think twice, as he had no way of knowing whether Hitler would endure in Germany as Mussolini had in Italy. However, Kearton's superior, Walter Hutchinson, believed that dictators, once firmly in the saddle, were hard to unseat, so he urged Kearton to go ahead with the purchase. Since no final decision could be reached until an outside authority was consulted, Kearton approached an acquaintance of his who could not only advise the firm on the merits of the work but could also do the necessary translation.

From February to April the sequence of events is a bit blurred. As a result of the reader's recommendation, Hurst & Blackett decided to accept Curtis Brown's price of £350 as an advance on royalties to Eher Verlag,[6] but before the contract could be drawn up and signed, E. T. S. Dugdale appeared at Kearton's office with his abridged translation tucked under his arm. He explained that he had learned of Hurst & Blackett's acquiring the rights to *Mein Kampf*, and since he had already been paid by the German publishers, he would like to offer it *gratis* to Hurst & Blackett. Apparently Dugdale had dealt directly with Eher Verlag who were satisfied with his version and put him in touch with Kearton. Somewhat surprised but nonetheless grateful, Hurst & Blackett accepted Dugdale's offer as it would allow them to publish the book much more quickly, and there was always the lurking fear that a shift in political fortunes would oust Hitler and make his autobiography superfluous. Also in the back of Walter Hutchinson's mind was his recently established printing works and the desirability of keeping it occupied.

Dugdale's version of *My Struggle* would soon have appeared but for the intrusion of Dr Hans Wilhelm Thost, the London correspondent for the official Nazi Party newspaper, *Völkischer Beobachter*. Most Englishmen at the time would not have known his name although he had lived and worked in London off and on since October 1930. He was familiar to the Home Office and the Foreign Office, however, because of the suspicious activities he engaged in.[7] Prominent within the Nazi organization in London, he sponsored speakers or delivered lectures himself which interpreted the aims and policies of the Nazis in a favourable light, and although he had no official diplomatic standing, he wielded great influence by maintaining close communication with high officials of the Nazi Party in Germany. Thus, when he suddenly informed

Kearton that Dugdale's translation would have to have the specific approval of the Nazi government despite the fact that the contract had already been signed and the abridgment was in galley proofs, Hurst & Blackett were stymied. They reluctantly released a copy to Thost who personally conveyed it to Berlin for official sanctioning, but when he returned he delivered a somewhat more expurgated text. As we shall see later, it is not possible to know which of Dugdale's passages were deleted, but there can be little doubt that further winnowing had taken place. In any case, Hurst & Blackett were finally allowed to go ahead, and Thost faded out of the picture. He remained in Britain two more years, in the end being expelled on suspicion of espionage. Before Dugdale's abridgment came out the following autumn, *The Times* was allowed to publish four extracts from his book. When these appeared at the end of July they provided the fullest exposure that English readers had yet had to the text of *Mein Kampf*.[8] By the October publication date people were eagerly anticipating the translation. No longer was there any doubt in Britain about Hitler's strength, and it was abundantly clear that the Nazis were firmly entrenched. The burning of the Reichstag and the emergency legislation of the previous spring had given Hitler dictatorial power for four years. In rapid succession the various political parties other than the National Socialists were outlawed. A successful Concordat with the Papacy undercut internal opposition from the Church. Already Jews were being deprived of their posts in the civil service, journalism, education, law, and medicine.

Once the volume appeared, the mood of anticipation gave way almost immediately to one of disappointment verging on hostility. Readers found it strange that the translation was anonymous, and had the American edition not mentioned Dugdale's name it would have been unknown for quite some time. It is not clear why Dugdale requested anonymity, but several alternatives suggest themselves. He naturally realized

7

that feelings ran high in Britain about Nazism, and he may have wished to avoid any guilt by association. He seems to have had great respect for Germany and her traditions, but little for Hitler and his cronies. Even when abridged, *My Struggle* contained obvious anti-semitic passages, and these might well have been embarrassing to his wife, who was so close to the Zionist cause.

Whatever the reasons, the absence of the translator's name gave rise to suspicion among reviewers. Ironically, it was one of Dugdale's good friends, the former *Times* correspondent and editor, Wickham Steed, who emphasized the point:

Herr Hitler may not know English, or understand English ways of feeling and thinking, well enough to perceive how sorry a service his Propaganda Department has rendered him in allowing his original volumes to be botched for English readers . . . As it is, any intelligent Nazi – if there be such – must be tempted to exclaim at the sight of the 280 expurgated pages of 'My Struggle': 'an enemy hath done this.'

Steed admitted that:

In justice to the anonymous translator (or Dr. Goebbels' Propaganda Department) it may be admitted that to compress the, roughly, 240,000 words of the German original into some 93,000 words of good English, would not have been easy in any event . . . [however] . . . Simply to skip the inner story of his boyhood, and to bowdlerise his, obviously truthful, account of the horror which certain aspects of life and vice in Viennese Jewry inspired in him, is to offer English readers dry bones instead of the breath of morbid life.[9]

The distinguished journalist and historian R. C. K. Ensor also felt that the anonymous translator had excluded too much: 'he seems to have omitted by-path details of German and Austrian politics and of Hitler's reaction to them, which perhaps he thought would bore English readers, but which really give most of the colour to the original book and are indispensable to a proper understanding of the Nazi mind'. Some commentators such as *The Times* went still further and suggested that there was an intentional glossing over and that 'the toning down appears to be deliberate'. A few years later a contributor to the *New York Times* was even more out-spoken: 'Some translations are again obviously edited with a view of softening the rough spots. The worst example of that lot is the English translation published in London.'[10]

To be sure, reviewers had some good things to point out as well. Speaking of Hitler's major foreign policy objectives, Ensor noted: 'these particular features come out clearly in the English abridgment'. *The Times* observed that 'the translation does not attempt to minimise Herr Hitler's anti-Semitism'. And a former American Ambassador to Germany commented: 'even in the abridged translation there are pages and pages of attacks upon the Jews'.[11]

Perhaps the most penetrating critique came not in the public press but in private correspondence. Shortly after *The Times* printed its four extracts from *Mein Kampf*, the head of the Zionist movement in Britain, Chaim Weizmann, protested in a private letter to the editor, Geoffrey Dawson:[12]

I personally have not the slightest apprehension as to the effect of Hitler's book on English readers if they are presented with it in its entirety. I have subjected myself to the painful task of reading it from cover to cover, and I can only say that in the whole of my reading I have never encountered a literary production so abominable. I have not the slightest doubt as to what the average Englishman who reads the book, as it stands, will think of these semi-manic perorations, these crude commonplaces, these pseudo-scientific biological and historical generalisations, just as I have little doubt about the verdict of any average neurologist on the mentality of their author.

Weizmann also enclosed a copy of another letter from his friend and fellow Zionist, Leonard Stein:

In the nature of things any kind of selection from Hitler's book involves an improvement of the original. In making any extracts on whatever topic and from whatever angle, the selector is inevitably led to choose the most concentrated and effective passages, but in doing so he of necessity conveys an entirely wrong impression of the literary character of the book. The reader who is offered these extracts can have no idea of the utter dreariness, of the incredible intellectual crudity of the original.

One of the most serious indictments against Dugdale's abridgment escaped the notice of his contemporaries. The book was printed in such a way as to make it almost impossible to detect where sections are left out or compressed. No ellipses are used and there are no annotations to indicate the extent of the deletions. Until 1939, when Houghton Mifflin authorized Reynal & Hitchcock of New York to bring out the whole work unabridged, anyone wishing to make a systematic comparison of Dugdale's abridgment with the full text was faced with a formidable task. However, the Reynal & Hitchcock edition used marginal notations to show which passages were being included for the first time. Comparing the two one can see the kinds of things Dugdale omitted, and perhaps guess at his reasons.

Dugdale frequently leaves out Hitler's tirades where he uses exaggerated phrases, an acerbic wit, and a coarse vernacular. Also missing is much of what Hitler originally said in Volume I, chapters 1–4, about Austria–Hungary. There is scarcely a mention of the Pan-Germanic movement in Austria or the Christian Socialist Party and its charismatic Viennese mayor, Karl Lueger. The squalor and distress of the Viennese working class and its susceptibility to trade unionism and Marxism have been censored. It almost seems as if the whole question of Austria was too sensitive, or more likely too tedious. Yet Germany's past and future greatness is scarcely left in doubt. Dugdale cites many passages where Hitler makes it clear that Germany must renounce her extra-territorial colonies and seek expansion on the European Continent. In chapter 4 of Volume I Hitler is quoted as saying: 'the sole hope of success for a territorial policy nowadays is to confine it to Europe, and not to extend it to places such as the Cameroons'.

A curious omission, however, is the following:

One must coolly and soberly accept the point of view that it certainly cannot be Heaven's intention to give fifty times as much land and soil of this earth to one nation as compared with another. In this case, political frontiers must not keep us away from the frontiers of eternal right. If this earth really has room for all to live in, then one should give us the space that we need for living.

And where might the Germans look to find a European state with fifty times the amount of land possessed by Germany? The abridgment is silent whereas the original text was explicit: 'If one wanted land and soil in Europe, then by and large this could only have been done at Russia's expense.' Preserved is Hitler's argument that Germany should have sought an alliance with Great Britain prior to 1914: 'For such a policy there was only one possible ally in Europe – Great Britain ... the only Power which could protect our rear, supposing we started a new Germanic expansion (*Germanenzug*).'

Hitler's attitude toward the Jews comes through clearly in the abridgment in chapters 2 and 10 of Volume I. Describing a chance encounter in Vienna, he contrasts his sheltered upbringing in Linz with the unfamiliar masses in the big city:

Once when I was walking through the inner city I suddenly came across a being in a long caftan with black side-locks. My first thought was: Is that a Jew? In Linz they did not look like that. I watched the man stealthily and cautiously, but the longer I stared at that strange countenance and studied it feature by feature, the more the question in a different form turned in my brain: Is that a German?

In spite of possible personal reticence, Dugdale doesn't shrink

11

from including Hitler's discussion of Zionism. However, almost without exception, the cruder expressions of anti-semitism are omitted:

In no other city of Western Europe could the relationship between Jewry and prostitution, and even now the white slave traffic, be studied better than in Vienna, with the possible exception of the sea ports of Southern France. . . An icy shudder ran down my spine when seeing for the first time the Jew as a cool, shameless, and calculating manager of this shocking vice, the outcome of the scum of the big city.

Also absent is Hitler's favourite anti-semitic theme of race pollution:

For hours the black-haired Jew boy, diabolic joy in his face, waits in ambush for the unsuspecting girl whom he defiles with his blood and thus robs her from her people. With the aid of all means he tries to ruin the racial foundations of the people to be enslaved.

In chapter 11 of Dugdale's version the familiar equation of Bolshevism with Judaism is also missing:

The most terrible example of this kind is offered by Russia where he [the Jew] killed or starved about thirty million people with a truly diabolic ferocity, under inhuman tortures, in order to secure to a crowd of Jewish scribblers and stock exchange robbers the rulership over a great people.

Hitler prided himself on his artistic and architectural expertise, yet most of his conservative views on these subjects are excluded from chapter 10. The following omission is typical:

He to whom this may seem strange should only subject to an examination the art of those States which have had the good fortune of being Bolshevized, and to his horror he will observe the sickly excrescences of lunatics or degenerate people which since the turn of the century we have learned to know under the collective conception of cubism or dadaism as the official art of those States.

In chapter 11 Dugdale sketches the broad outlines of Hitler's theory that nations, like species in nature, must struggle for existence, and that the Aryan race is the bearer or perpetuator of higher culture. But Hitler's more detailed pseudo-scientific views about population growth and the impact of syphilis on modern society are absent. So are the more explicit sentences like: 'Just as little as Nature desires a mating between weaker individuals and stronger ones, far less she desires the mixing of a higher race with a lower one, as in this case her entire work of higher breeding, which has perhaps taken hundreds of thousands of years, would tumble at one blow.' Hitler's comments about blacks are also expurgated:

From time to time it is demonstrated to the German petty *bourgeois* in illustrated periodicals that for the first time here or there a negro has become a lawyer, teacher, even clergyman, or even a leading opera tenor or something of that kind . . . that it is a criminal absurdity to train a born half-ape until one believes a lawyer has been made of him, while millions of members of the highest culture race have to remain in entirely unworthy positions; that it is a sin against the will of the eternal Creator to let hundreds and hundreds of thousands of His most talented beings degenerate in the proletarian swamp of today, while Hottentots and Zulu Kafirs are trained for intellectual vocations.

What emerges from a comparison of the two texts is largely a difference of style. The small graphic details which give colour and texture to Hitler's narrative are missing in Dugdale's translation; with the rough edges deleted, Hitler appears less a fanatic and more of a shrewd politician. Above all, he is presented so as not to appear ridiculous in the eyes of foreigners. Notwithstanding this whitewash, Hitler's main ideas and policies remain intact, including foreign expansion in the future; the rebuilding of German idealism and self-confidence; Germany's need for strong leadership; the need to manipulate the mass electorate through propaganda; the eternal struggle against Bolshevism and the Jews; the ultimate repudiation of the Treaty of Versailles; and the role which the Nazis hoped to play in the rebirth of the German state.

Having said this, the question still persists whether Dugdale sufficiently appreciated the Nazi menace. Just how careful an observer of contemporary Germany was he? Was there an element of naïveté when it came to editing *Mein Kampf*? He himself answers some of these uncertainties in an article he published in the *English Review* of October 1931.[13] Although one can't say for certain, it is very likely that 'National Socialism in Germany' was prompted by his work on the as yet unpublished abridgment.

The article is an assessment of Hitler's aims and prospects as presented in *Mein Kampf*, and as such constitutes one of the better summaries in the press of the day. Dugdale's treatment is neither naïve nor simplistic, and there is certainly nothing to suggest a cover-up. He admits that it would be hard to predict how Hitler would act if he ever came to power. Like many others, he wondered if a Nazi victory at the polls would pave the way for a Communist uprising, or alternatively might make Hitler more moderate and reasonable. Above all Dugdale fully appreciated 'Herr Hitler's conviction that nothing but a personal dictatorship can set the new ideal going in Germany whilst those who are to administer the country must owe the dictator unquestioning obedience and be deeply imbued with his spirit'. On foreign policy Dugdale concluded: 'France is the eternal enemy, and the result of the War has been to make her the paramount Power in Europe. Since neither England nor Italy can possibly desire permanence for this condition of things, England and Italy are Germany's most natural allies . . . Russia would be fatal as an ally for Germany.'

In all of this Dugdale was not averse to promoting, in a

14

back-handed sort of way, his own translation of Hitler's
autobiography.

The book that sets forth these ideals has had a vast sale all over
Germany among the younger members both of the educated and
working classes. Its propaganda has penetrated deep into a nation
which is but too ready to accept any ideas, if only they are presented with sufficient force behind them.

Mein Kampf has, however, not so far been put before the public
in this country in any form, complete or abridged. When we consider that it is implicitly believed in by a large section of the
German people, it seems not unimportant that English readers
should get to know what the National Socialists intend to effect
in Germany, if ever they get the chance.

Insofar as his translation of *Mein Kampf* is concerned one can
hardly accuse Dugdale of not assessing the Nazi movement
adequately. As early as 1931 he was very much alive to its
policies and intentions and therefore some of the most blatant
omissions in his abridgment are almost certainly the result of
Dr Thost's tardy and unexpected intervention. Although
many critics of the translation blamed Dugdale for ignoring
Hitler's references to France, Cherry Kearton specifically
recalls that among the last-minute changes wrought by the
German government were passages having to do with France
and with anti-semitism.

If Dugdale was not responsible for all the shortcomings of
the Hurst & Blackett edition of 1933, was there anything
which the London publishers could have done to resist Dr
Thost's demands? The agreement with Eher Verlag makes it
clear that there was not. Hurst & Blackett, in one sense, had
bargained away more than they had realized in return for the
convenience of using Dugdale's abridgment. According to the
contract, Eher Verlag merely undertook to supply 'a competent English translation', and beyond this they stipulated that
the volume could be further abridged but not expanded.

Control over the text, therefore, ultimately remained with the Nazis.

This being the case, we begin to understand why there was a delay in publication, and the reasons for the confusion concerning who would translate *Mein Kampf*, as well as what would or would not be included. One question remains. Did Hitler's publishers really expect that they could indefinitely prevent a full English text from appearing? As we shall see later, Hurst & Blackett's unabridged edition of 1939 would not have official Nazi permission.[14]

As anticipated, sales of the first English-language translation were brisk.[15] The first edition of 5,000 was sold out by the end of 1933. It was a de luxe version, selling for 18s., and it was never reprinted again. Almost simultaneously a popular edition was marketed at 3s. 6d., and by the end of the year sales of this cheaper volume had reached 10,687.[16]

Hurst & Blackett lost no time fulfilling their contract obligations to Eher Verlag, and in November 1933 paid them £350 in advance of royalties. However, before the money reached Munich, Curtis Brown deducted 20% commission as literary agent, and the Inland Revenue took its share of £84.7s. leaving the German firm with a net advance of £195.13s. or RM2,611.

As can be seen in the following table, sales of the abridgment tapered off slightly between 1934 and 1936.[17]

Year	On Hand	Editions Printed	Sales	Gross Royalties	Commission	Tax	Net Royalties
1934	1,275	9th–10th: 3,500	4,696	£76.1.2	£15.4.4		£58.5.9 or RM715
1935	79	11th–12th: 3,500	2,989	£74.18.6	£14.19.8	£7.3.0	£52.15.10 or RM653
1936	590	13th–16th: 7,000	3,633	£243.14.1	£48.14.10	£36.17.5	£158.1.10 or RM1,941

From the number of copies printed in 1936 it is clear that the publishers were counting on markedly increased sales, due no doubt to the tension building up in Germany over the military occupation of the Rhineland and the restoration of conscription. However, sales remained steady and began to pick up only during the course of 1937 when in June an additional 2,496 were sold, and later a further 6,152 were found buyers. Only 1,750 copies were printed for the 17th impression, but 5,000 were run off for the 18th. Thus, on the eve of 1938, the fateful year of the Anschluss with Austria and the Munich Agreement, a total of 35,547 copies had been sold, 148 complimentary copies dispersed, and 2,055 remained on hand.

Sales figures for 1938 surpassed all expectations, amounting to almost seven times the previous year. To meet the demand, Hurst & Blackett printed 5,000 for both the 19th and 20th impressions, increasing the number to 7,750 for the 21st and 22nd. By 30 June, 11,592 copies had been sold, and the decision was made to supplement the popular edition with a slightly more expensive 5s. library edition. At the end of December the popular edition showed an additional 14,815 sales and the library edition 27,331, making the year's total 53,738, of which slightly over 8,000 were colonial sales. The abridgment had therefore sold 89,285 by the end of 1938, more than twice the number of copies imagined by contemporaries and later scholars.

Eher Verlag's royalties for 1937–8 finally began to keep pace with the augmented sales.

6 months ending	Gross Royalties	Commission	Tax	Net Royalties	
30 June 1937	£82.19.8	£17.19.6	£12.13.3	£53.14.11	or RM681
31 Dec. 1937	£91.2.9	£18.4.7	£11.15.1	£61.3.1	or RM793
30 June 1938	£181.1.4	£36.4.2	£30.11.4	£114.5.10	or RM1,320
31 Dec. 1938	£856.13.8	£171.6.8	£163.8.10	£521.18.2	or RM6,090

Captured German records cease to exist for royalties after 31 December 1938, due to the outbreak of war in September 1939. We know that there were 16,442 copies on hand at the beginning of 1939, and one would probably be safe in assuming that these plus many more were sold.

As far as we can tell, Hurst & Blackett phased out the 3s. 6d. edition and concentrated on the 5s. one, supplementing it in March 1939 with a translation of the full text. From then on, Dugdale's abridgment presumably fell out of favour as customers scrambled to purchase the 'unexpurgated' version. Prior to the war, the abridgment probably realized sales of 100,000. With the adult population of Britain numbering about 25 million, one copy was available for every 250 men and women; and though the book may not always have been read, it was clearly in evidence.

Book reviews are only a crude measure of exposure, but the following list, alphabetically arranged, shows how widely Dugdale's translation was noticed when it appeared.[18] *Birmingham Gazette* (13 Oct. 1933); *Birmingham Post* (13 Oct.); *Daily Express* (13 Oct.); *Daily Herald* (13 Oct.); *Daily Mail* (13 Oct.); *Daily Sketch* (13 Oct.); *Daily Telegraph* (13 Oct.); *Evening News* (13 Oct.); *Evening Standard* (13 Oct.); *Everyman* (13 Oct.); *Irish Independent* (13 Oct.); *Leeds Mercury* (13 Oct.); *Listener* (17 Jan. 1934); *Liverpool Post* (13 Oct. 1933); *Manchester Guardian* (13 Oct.); *Morning Post* (13 Oct.); *New Britain* (18 Oct.); *News Chronicle* (13 Oct.); *Northern Echo* (13 Oct.); *Nottingham Guardian* (13 Oct.); *Observer* (15 Oct.); *Oxford Times* (20 Oct.); *Public Opinion* (20 Oct.); *Punch* (8 Nov.); *Reynolds News* (15 Oct.); *Scotsman* (19 Oct.); *Spectator* (20 Oct.); *Star* (13 Oct.); *Sunday Dispatch* (15 Oct.); *The Times* (13 and 23 Oct.); *The Times Literary Supplement* (19 Oct.); *Time and Tide* (21 Oct.); *Western Morning News* (13 Oct.); *Yorkshire Herald* (13 Oct.); *Yorkshire Post* (18 Oct.).

Dugdale's abridgment clearly received considerable public exposure, which inevitably raises the question whether or not *Mein Kampf* was a valid key to Hitler's ultimate intentions. If, as some say, it was merely the emotional and confused reactions of a madman to events of the 1920s, then any amount of abridging would not matter. On the other hand, if the book actually embodied a long-range blueprint for aggression, as those who pointed to such events as the repudiation of the Treaty of Versailles, the military rearmament of Germany, the reoccupation of the Rhineland, the Anschluss with Austria, and the recovery of the Sudetenland, claimed, then an abridgment could be edited so as to obscure Hitler's aims. One must also recognize that in contrast to Hitler's professed goals he also indulged in an equal number of contradictory actions which were not anticipated in *Mein Kampf*. These would include his pact with Poland in 1934; the rapprochement with the non-Aryan Japanese; the willingness to leave Italy in possession of the Tyrol; German military assistance to Franco during the Spanish Civil War; the Nazi–Soviet pact of 1939; and the provoking of war with Great Britain. Lastly, if Hitler was the consummate opportunist, why would he feel bound in the 1930s by anything written ten years previously?

By 1938–9 the British were more than casually interested in Hitler's next moves. Supplementing Dugdale's translation were a host of books and articles seeking to predict coming events. Newspapers abounded with up-to-date releases, and broadcasters regularly forecast the news together with its analysis. Far from being oblivious to Hitler, many in Britain were all too aware of his hates and aspirations, and because they took *Mein Kampf* literally they not only sighed with relief when Hitler turned his attention away from France and focused it on the annexation of Austria, but also believed him when he threatened to invade Czechoslovakia and therefore rejoiced about Chamberlain's Munich detente. Trusting that German expansion was going to proceed predictably eastward, they were dumbfounded by the signing of the Nazi–Soviet pact in August 1939, as nothing in *Mein Kampf*'s pages even hinted at such an agreement.

Further complicating the task of Hitler-watchers was his habit of making speeches or policy statements that seemed to contradict what he had said in *Mein Kampf*, and those who had access to the full text, including the Germans themselves, were frequently no better off in divining Hitler's intentions than people who had read only the abridgment. If some were taken in by Hitler, it was because they were so predisposed, and if others discerned his villainy it was undoubtedly because they intrinsically distrusted him. Both positions could be buttressed by reading either the full or the abridged text.

II

The British Foreign Office and *Mein Kampf*

In considering the impact of *Mein Kampf* on British government circles during the 1930s, three questions suggest themselves. First, did the Foreign Office pay much attention to *Mein Kampf*? Second, did foreign policy experts ever seek to predict Hitler's future course of action on the basis of statements in *Mein Kampf*? Finally, did Neville Chamberlain and his immediate coterie of advisers shamefully neglect the insights to be gained from a familiarity with Hitler's autobiography?

The first of these queries is the easiest to answer, since the Foreign Office was thoroughly alerted to the implications of *Mein Kampf* within three months of Hitler's becoming Chancellor. On 26 April 1933 the British Ambassador in Berlin, Sir Horace Rumbold, addressed a lengthy dispatch to the British Foreign Secretary, Sir John Simon.[1] In *Mein Kampf*, Hitler showed considerable admiration for the way in which the Allies used propaganda against the Germans during the First World War:

He displays a cynical and at the same time a very clear understanding of the psychology of the German masses. He knows what he has achieved with oratory and cheap sentiment during the last fourteen years by his own unaided efforts. Now that he has the resources of the State at his disposal, he has good reason to believe that he can mould public opinion to his views to an unprecedented extent. After all, his recent victory is the best proof that the methods which he proposes to adopt [in *Mein Kampf*] are sound.

21

Rumbold then proceeded to discuss the 'principles' which had 'guided' Hitler since 1918:

Stripped of the verbiage in which he has clothed it, Hitler's thesis is extremely simple. He starts with the assertions that man is a fighting animal; therefore the nation is, he concludes, a fighting unit, being a community of fighters. Any living organism which ceases to fight for its existence is, he asserts, doomed to extinction. A country or race which ceases to fight is equally doomed. The fighting capacity of a race depends on its purity. Hence the necessity for ridding it of foreign impurities. The Jewish race, owing to its universality, is of necessity pacifist and internationalist. Pacifism is the deadliest sin, for pacifism means a surrender of the race in the fight for existence. The first duty of every country is, therefore, to nationalise the masses; intelligence is of secondary importance in the case of the individual; will and determination are of higher importance. The individual who is born to command is more valuable than countless thousands of subordinate natures.

The aim of education, according to *Mein Kampf*, was to prepare young men for their future role as soldiers, and in turn to convince the army of its invincibility against all of Germany's foes. As Hitler himself declared:

Give the German nation 6 millions of young men perfectly trained by athletics, consumed by fanatical patriotism, educated to the maximum of aggressiveness, and a national State will, if necessary, be able to convert them in less than two years into a regular army, provided certain cadres are available . . . To forge the necessary weapons is the task of the internal political leaders of the people. To see that the weapon can be forged and to find allies is the task of the Minister for Foreign Affairs. Foreign policy may be unscrupulous. It is not the task of diplomacy to allow a nation to founder heroically but rather to see that it can prosper and survive. There are only two possible allies for Germany – England and Italy . . . Germany's lost provinces cannot be gained by solemn appeals to Heaven or by pious hopes in the League of Nations, but only by force of arms.

Sir Horace alleged that Hitler was prepared to abandon pre-war German colonial ambitions in favour of territorial expansion in the direction of Russia and the Baltic states, but he cautioned:

How far Hitler is prepared to put his fantastic proposals into operation is of course uncertain, but it is clear that he cannot abandon the cardinal points of his programme any more than Lenin or Mussolini could. They are, he declares, the granite pillars on which his policy is supported. He asserts again and again that they cannot be altered or modified.

The tasks facing the new Nazi regime were complicated, and presented challenges regarding strategy and tactics:

They have to rearm on land, and, as Herr Hitler explains in his memoirs, they have to lull their adversaries into such a state of coma that they will allow themselves to be engaged one by one. It may seem astonishing that the Chancellor should express himself so frankly, but it must be noted that his book was written in 1925, when his prospects of reaching power were so remote that he could afford to be candid. He would probably be glad to suppress every copy extant today. Since he assumed office, Herr Hitler has been as cautious and discreet as he was formerly blunt and frank. He declares that he is anxious that peace should be maintained for a ten year period. What he probably means can be more accurately expressed by the formula: Germany needs peace until she has recovered such strength that no country can challenge her without serious and irksome preparations.

Rumbold's lengthy dispatch was circulated among the members of the Cabinet and also sent to the Prime Minister, Ramsay MacDonald. A few months afterwards, *The Times* reprinted extracts from the forthcoming Dugdale abridged translation of *Mein Kampf*. As we saw in the previous chapter, Chaim Weizmann wrote to the editor of *The Times*, Geoffrey Dawson, complaining that they were not representative of the original German version. Weizmann sent a copy of this letter

23

together with its enclosures to the Foreign Office as well. To Dawson he lamented:[2]

It is all the more distressing to find that by the method of careful selection employed, a number of fairly plausible passages have been arranged to give the impression to the English reader of *The Times* – who will not touch the book – that Hitler is a perhaps rather radical, but on the whole by no means unreasonable political thinker and agitator. I find it very painful to say so, but I am sure that anyone who reads the leading article in last Monday's *Times* can hardly help feeling that some such impression has already been made on at least one, and certainly most competent, reader of these extracts. The air of plausibility with which Hitler's allegations against the Jews are invested in the leading article's summary, the suggestion inevitably conveyed by it that Hitler's barbarism is something in the nature of a healthy reaction against a sordid and unmanly sexualism, attributed largely to the Jews, ... all these must lead the reader of *The Times* ... to see the Nazi creed in a much more favourable light.

Weizmann sent 28 pages of translated extracts from the original edition of *Mein Kampf* to Dawson in hopes that he would reprint some of them in *The Times* as an antidote to the Dugdale selections. In spite of Dawson's refusal to use them, the Foreign Office – also the beneficiary of these extracts – placed them all on file. The bulk of the passages contained semi-obscene allegations against the Jews, but in addition there were quotations reflecting Hitler's views on foreign policy:

That the re-conquest of the frontiers of 1914 could only be achieved by war no-one will hardly doubt. Only childish and naive minds can lull themselves into the belief that the Treaty of Versailles may be revised by such slinking and begging methods – quite apart from the fact that such an effort would require a Talleyrand nature which we do not possess ... Times have changed since the Vienna Congress: not princes and royal mistresses bargain for frontiers, but the irreconcilable world Jew fights for his dominion over the

24

nations. No people can remove that fist from its throat except by the sword.

National Socialism, however, demanded more than merely the restoration of pre-war frontiers and the destruction of the peace treaties: 'Therefore we National Socialists put an end to the foreign policy of pre-war days ... we stop the Germanic march to the South and West and direct our eyes to the land in the East . . . if we speak today of new soil in Europe we can only think of Russia and the border States subjected to it.' Hitler acknowledged that the other European powers might resist German expansion, and so he proffered advice accordingly:

The political testament of the German Nation for its foreign policy must always be the following. Never tolerate the rise of two Continental Powers in Europe. Regard every attempt to organize a second military power on the frontiers of Germany – even if it only be the establishment of a state which is capable of becoming a military power – as an attack against Germany. Regard it not merely as your right, but as your duty to use every weapon, and even arms, for preventing the development of such states, or for destroying them if they have already arisen.

As the best means of undercutting France's position on the Continent, Hitler advocated an Anglo–German–Italian rapprochement. Finally, the extracts which Weizmann supplied to the editor of *The Times* highlighted the role of education in the Nazi programme:

The entire educational and cultural system of the National State must have as its supreme culmination the burning into the mind and heart of the youth entrusted to it the sense of race, both through instinct and through reason. No boy and no girl should leave school without having been led to the ultimate realisation of the necessity and the meaning of the purity of blood.

By mixing with other races we lift these up from their present level to a higher one, but we ourselves sink down from our own heights for all eternity. This education from the point of view of race must find its ultimate completion in military service, as indeed military service should form the completion of the normal education of the average German.

For the next two years the Foreign Office formally ignored *Mein Kampf*, but in the latter half of 1935 and first half of 1936, it took a renewed interest. In part this was stimulated by Alfred Rosenberg's eulogistic article in *Völkischer Beobachter* for 18 July 1935, which celebrated the tenth anniversary of *Mein Kampf*'s publication. The book was, according to Rosenberg, the 'unshakeable basis of National Socialist feeling and thought'.[3] In a note to his colleagues at the Foreign Office, Michael Creswell commented:

I have ventured to have this article by Rosenberg in the Völkischer Beobachter entered [in the Foreign Office archives], since it seems to have been recently portended that some of the extreme doctrines enunciated in 'Mein Kampf' are no longer held by Herr Hitler. This bombastic article by the Reich 'Culture' leader should show that the German Ministers at any rate have no doubt on that score! And nor need we, if we judge by Hitler's deeds rather than by his words.

Another reason for *Mein Kampf* again coming to the attention of the Foreign Office was the flurry created by Katharine Ramsay, Duchess of Atholl. Elected to Parliament as a Conservative in 1924, she served as Parliamentary Secretary to the Board of Education for the next five years, and only gradually thereafter began to take an interest in foreign policy. In the autumn of 1935 she had occasion to discuss *Mein Kampf* with Rennie Smith, a former Labour Party M.P., who had devoted the past few years to exposing the menace of Nazism through an organization called the Friends of Europe. Smith had enlisted the aid of leading scholars and statesmen in the preparation of over thirty pamphlets dealing with various aspects of German domestic

26

and foreign policy. Years later, in his unpublished memoirs, he described his meeting with the Duchess:

It happened that at the time I had just completed the draft of a new pamphlet based on Hitler's 'Mein Kampf', from which I had extracted and translated all that was concerned with his ideas of German foreign policy . . . I suggested that she might like to read this draft . . . In a day or two she was back again – horrified. 'I had no idea that he was that sort of man,' she said. I invited her – she seemed to me to be qualifying for the job – to write a Foreword to the draft she had just read. She accepted. Her Foreword was one of the longest and 'most considered' which 'Friends of Europe' published. The pamphlet, too, was printed, re-printed, and distributed in larger quantities than any other 'Friends of Europe' pamphlet.

The stages by which the Duchess of Atholl became involved in the project are not entirely clear, for her version differs somewhat from that of Smith. It is clear that she came to view herself as the guiding spirit of pamphlet no. 38 in the series. In her autobiography she wrote:[4]

A neighbour of ours in Chelsea, Miss Nesti Sanders, who was a good German scholar and a member of a National Citizens Union, had shown me certain passages in Hitler's book, *Mein Kampf*. In them he had made clear that his policy was an unashamedly aggressive one. I had just read a recently published English translation of the book, and I was horrified to find that it was only about one-third the length of the original, and that all the bellicose passages had been so watered down as to have lost their meaning. I asked the Librarian of the Foreign Office to give me official translations of these passages but was told, to my surprise, that none had been made.

Her inquiry was made by telephone to Sir Stephen Gaselee on 5 December 1935. After looking through his office files, he replied:[5]

I find that we never actually instituted a comparison of the German and English editions in order to find out exactly what was omitted in the latter. I have a faint memory that there was something of this kind in *The Times* and I expect that the Librarian of the House of Commons could dig this out for you if necessary.

We did however have sent to us the translation of a series of the most outrageous passages in the German edition and our correspondent said (doubtless with truth) that these or most of them would certainly be omitted in the translation meant for British readers. I send you herewith this little collection hoping that it may be of use to you. A comparison with the English edition should very soon show which are there and which are not.

As this is my only copy of these passages I shall be grateful if Your Grace will return them to me when you have done with them.

Resuming her account of the episode, the Duchess recalled:

Encouraged by Wickham Steed, *The Times* former editor, I therefore accepted an invitation from a Labour Member to contribute to a series of pamphlets he was publishing in which authoritative translations would be given of the more alarming passages in *Mein Kampf*. I set to work on this at once.

The selections from *Mein Kampf* with which Sir Stephen Gaselee supplied the Duchess of Atholl were the ones that Weizmann had given the Foreign Office two years before. Writing from Blair Castle in Perthshire on 7 January 1936, the Duchess thanked Gaselee for the loan of the extracts, a portion of which she copied:[6]

These passages are, as you say, outrageous and the worst of them are certainly omitted from the English translation. I notice, as a matter of fact, that your extracts are not always complete, and do not always indicate that they are not complete. Would it not be rather valuable if a comparison could be made between the German and English editions in order to find out exactly what is omitted in the latter? If 'Mein Kampf' were no longer being published in full in Germany it would not matter so much, but I have recently bought a copy in two volumes, the first volume of which is dated 1934 and the second 1935, and I am told that it is recommended in the Hitler Press as a book that should be in every German household. A very-well informed person was also told by a German official two years ago that all officials had to have it. We cannot therefore regard it as out of date, and it seems to me very misleading to the British public that a book which, so far as I can see, leaves out all the passages in which a definite policy of a very dangerous kind is laid down, should have a wide circulation. I find that ten editions of the English translation were published between October 1933 and October 1935, although the book cost 18/–. Its price is now reduced to 5/–, and its circulation is likely to be enormously increased.

As a matter of fact I have just been informed that the English translation is being sold on the bookstalls at quite small stations, and has found its way to Perthshire.

I quite understand that the Foreign Office would not wish to publish a comparison of the two editions, but would it not be desirable that such a comparison should be made for the use of the Office?

The following day Gaselee acknowledged her return of the extracts, and said he would call to the attention of his colleagues her suggestion of making a comparison between the two editions. 'I am sure it would be valuable. It is really a question of staff and time.'[7]

During the next few days various members of the Central Department of the Foreign Office commented on the Duchess' proposal.[8] One noted:

It is very doubtful whether Central Department have time, at present, to make a proposed comparison between the German and English editions of 'Mein Kampf'. The Duchess of Atholl suggests that such a comparison might be useful to the Foreign Office. One difficulty is, however, that if we institute the comparison here, it can hardly be published, and thus the real point of such a comparison – i.e. the enlightenment of the public – would be missed.

29

Another observed:

I agree. I presume that it is generally known (among the informed) that the English edition of 'Mein Kampf' differs from the original German version – but it is rather difficult to suggest how this can be brought home to the uninformed. The existing English edition is presumably 'approved' by Hitler: and to bring out a rather different edition, *not* authorized by Hitler, might expose the publisher to difficulties with the law. No doubt the News Department have brought this matter to the attention of press correspondents.

The point raised in this last comment is significant, for there is no evidence that either the Duchess of Atholl or the Friends of Europe intended to secure permission in order to expose the discrepancies between the two editions.

The Duchess of Atholl's inquiry also piqued Sir Stephen Gaselee's own interest, and a week after she had telephoned, he decided to examine the Foreign Office's only copy of the original German version of *Mein Kampf.* To his great chagrin he found that the volumes were missing. During his efforts to locate them someone suggested that they might have been inadvertently carried off to Peking![9] When this proved not so it was suggested that Orme Sargent might have them. Four months later the missing tomes were indeed found in Sargent's possession in London, but in the meantime a second copy was ordered through the British Embassy in Berlin.

For his part Sargent had been busily perusing *Mein Kampf* and on 2 April 1936 he addressed the following request to Sir Eric Phipps, British Ambassador to Germany:[10]

I was wondering whether it would be possible for someone at the Embassy to prepare a short memorandum giving such extracts from 'Mein Kampf' (i.e. the edition at present circulating in Germany), as are in more or less flagrant contradiction with Hitler's recent offers and assurances in the matter of foreign policy. If such extracts do not appear in the expurgated English

30

translation of 'Mein Kampf' so much the better. Indeed the fact might be noted in the memorandum.

Such a memorandum would be very useful to us just at this moment: and the Embassy is probably better qualified to compile it than anyone here.

Phipps was somewhat dubious. It would be a large under-taking for his Embassy staff, especially if the comparison included a correlation with Hitler's recent speeches. Further-more, the Embassy in Berlin didn't have a copy of the Dugdale translation. Were such a Memorandum prepared, Phipps believed that it would be unwise to attach much importance to it:[11]

If you want to use it in debate, the Germans will always answer, as Blomberg did to me, that it is unfair to take the foreign affairs passages of 'Mein Kampf' literally and that reference should be made to Hitler's present-day speeches for information as to his present ideas on foreign policy. If, on the other hand, you wish to form a judgment as to the sincerity of Hitler's recent offers, 'Mein Kampf' is also dangerous. The book doubtless represents in the main Hitler's ideas and ideals. But, as he has himself said, it is sometimes necessary to bow to the inevitable and deviate from ones course. The Polish Agreement [1934] is a case in point. It is therefore possible that Hitler, whilst seeking ultimately the goals described in 'Mein Kampf', is genuinely prepared to agree to a 25-year truce. It may also be that he is insincere in offering this truce, but it would be dangerous to rely on 'Mein Kampf' to decide the point.

Phipps went on to describe an episode during which Göring alluded to *Mein Kampf* as his Bible, and when asked to explain, 'Göring pretended that "Mein Kampf" was only his Bible for internal and not external affairs! The fact is the Germans want to do that almost impossible thing (even with old English ladies and Bishops) viz., to deceive everybody *all the time*.'

Despite Phipps' reservations about preparing a Memorandum, the Embassy in Berlin went ahead with the project, as reported by Ivone Kirkpatrick. 'The English edition which I had never seen before is the most miserable précis of the German version and in many places does not purport to be a translation.'[12] Several weeks later this was followed by the completed document which bore the title: *Central, Germany, 7 May 1936 – Confidential – A Translation of Some of the More Important Passages from Hitler's Mein Kampf* (*1925 Edition*) prepared by H.M. Embassy, Berlin. This Memorandum consisted of eleven closely printed pages[13] and included many of the key passages omitted from the Dugdale translation.

One of the most characteristic features of *Mein Kampf* was Hitler's use of Social Darwinism to justify his brutal instincts:

The role of the strongest is to dominate and not to mingle himself with the weaker, thus sacrificing his own greatness. Only the weak by birth can consider this law to be cruel; but such a one is but a weak and limited man; for if this law were not to win the day, the evolution of all organised beings would be inconceivable.

The natural implication of a doctrine based on struggle and survival was, according to Hitler, the waging of war:

When nations struggle for their existence on this planet and the question is raised whether they shall survive or not, all humanitarian and aesthetic considerations are of no avail, for conceptions of this kind are not of the world, but come out of the imaginations of men and are bound to that imagination . . . As regards the humanitarian question, Moltke already has explained himself thereon, taking the view that in war humanitarianism consists in executing it with the utmost possible rapidity, and that as a consequence the most brutal methods are the most humanitarian.

Hitler was also fond of repeating over and over again that in history as well as in biology what mattered was the survival of the strongest race as distinct from a particular state or form of government:

The British Foreign Office and *Mein Kampf*

In general it must never be forgotten that it is not the highest aim of man's existence to maintain a State or, indeed, a Government, but rather to preserve its national character.

If the latter is in danger of being oppressed or removed, then the question of legality plays only a subordinate part. It may be that the ruling power a thousandfold employs so-called 'legal' methods in its proceedings, but, nevertheless, the impulse to self-preservation of the oppressed nation is always the best justification for its fight with all weapons . . .

The rights of man break the rights of States.

If, in a struggle for human rights, a race goes under, it means that it has weighed too light in the scales of fate to be fit to continue in this world. For if a man is unprepared or unable to fight for his life, just Providence has already decreed his end.

The world is not for cowardly peoples.

The Foreign Office Memorandum dealt not only with the abstract passages concerning aggression but focused on very concrete subjects as well. The uniting of all Germans under one Reich was a major theme, otherwise referred to as Pan-Germanism. Yet the realization of this policy would inevitably disrupt the peace of Europe and destroy the Treaty of Versailles.

The idea of re-establishing the 1914 frontiers is a piece of political insanity both in its nature and in its consequences which make it a veritable crime. This can be said without recalling that the frontiers of the Reich in 1914 were anything but logical. In reality they did not group all men of German nationality and they were no more rational from the strategic point of view. . . The frontiers of 1914 are without any value for the future of the German nation. They were neither a safeguard in the past nor a force for the future . . . On the contrary, we National Socialists must hold unshakenly to the end of our foreign policy that of assuring to the German people the territory which is its on earth; and this action is the only one which, before God and before our German posterity can justify the shedding of blood. Before God, since we were put on this earth to gain there our daily bread by means of perpetual conflict as

33

creatures to whom nothing was given save as the result of sacrifice and who will owe their situation of masters of the world only to the intelligence and courage with which they know how to conquer and maintain it; before our German posterity in so much as the blood of not one single German citizen will be shed without giving to the future Germany thousands of new citizens. The territory, on which the vigorous children of generations of German peasants will one day multiply, will justify the sacrifice of our own blood and absolve the responsible statesmen, persecuted perhaps even by their own generation, for the bloodshed and the sacrifice imposed on our nation.

The Memorandum also emphasized the familiar theme of *Lebensraum*, which led many observers to label Nazism as the heir of Prussian expansionism:

The frontiers of Germany are fortuitous and temporary limits in the course of the eternal political struggle; it is the same with the frontiers delimiting the habitations of other nations . . . The boundaries of states are the work of men and are changed by them. The fact that a nation has succeeded in acquiring the territory in excess of its requirements in no way confers a superior obligation to admit that forever. It is a demonstration rather of the force of the conqueror and the weakness of him who admits conquest. And it is in that force alone that right resides . . . In the same way in the future it is no racial grace which will give land to our nation and with it the means of existence, but only the power of the victorious sword can obtain it.

One of the enduring criticisms of the Dugdale translation was its omission of menacing statements about France. To counteract this, the Memorandum inserted several:

If the German nation wishes to put an end to a state of affairs which threatens to remove it from Europe, it must not recommit the error committed before the War and make enemies of the whole world; it must distinguish its most dangerous enemy, so as to strike with concentrated force against him . . .

Just as we are all today convinced of the necessity of having it out with France, so even that would be inefficacious for us if the objectives of our foreign policy were limited to that. One could only interpret that as a means of covering our rear in order to expand our utmost in Europe.

Finally, although conflict leading to war was deemed inevitable, and the strongest race was destined to win, paradoxically the result would be peace:

If the German people had possessed in the course of its history that unity which was so useful to other peoples, the German Reich would today be master of the globe. The history of the world would have taken another course, and no one can now decide if humanity would not, in following that course, have reached the goal to which so many blinded pacifists hope today to arrive by their quibbling and trivial talk, a peace not assured by the olive branches which, with facile tears, the weeping pacifists wave, but guaranteed by the victorious sword of a master people, who put the entire world at the service of a superior civilization.

The head of the Central Department of the Foreign Office, Ralph Wigram, was very pleased with this Memorandum, and suggested that the Confidential Print be circulated to the Cabinet. Another of his colleagues noted: 'An excellent and most useful paper. Give to it the fullest circulation that may be considered advisable. It should in my opinion be the widest possible.'[14] This was done, as Anthony Eden, the Foreign Secretary, later recalled:[15]

At my request, our Embassy there [Berlin] and the Central Department at the Foreign Office prepared a summary of Hitler's odious creed in a Memorandum of eleven pages, liberally illustrated with revealing extracts from *Mein Kampf*. At least there should be no pretext that unpleasant realities were not exposed to those with whom responsibility lay.

The last sentence was directed at the Prime Minister, according to Ralph Wigram's widow. 'It was written primarily for the benefit of Stanley Baldwin, whom Ralph Wigram thought was very unaware of the German menace.'[16]

Curiously enough, the same Memorandum, prompted by the queries and urgings of the Duchess of Atholl, may well have provided her with additional illustrations for her own pamphlet. Just as she was about to go to press, members of the Foreign Office suggested sharing the contents of the Memorandum with her.[17] On 16 May Gaselee noted:

You may recollect my correspondence a few months ago with the Duchess of Atholl about 'Mein Kampf'. She is very anxious to call the attention of the British public to it in all its original savagery, and I believe is writing or editing a pamphlet to that end. Her material is not complete, and she is anxious for more. Do you think it would be proper to send her this section of Confidential Print for use and ultimate return?

The same day Wigram commented:

I am all for her using it. She can use practically all of this except the passages marked on pages 5 and 7. Any member of the public could have written it. We might see her proof privately if she likes. I've a lot more stuff I could give her extracted from German speeches.

Whether the Duchess of Atholl saw the Foreign Office Memorandum before sending her pamphlet to the printers is uncertain, but internal evidence would suggest that she did. A copy of the pamphlet, entitled *Germany's Foreign Policy as Stated in Mein Kampf by Adolf Hitler*, with a Foreword by the Duchess of Atholl, M.P., was received by the Foreign Office Library on 18 June. An Introductory Note sketched briefly the Duchess's career, emphasizing that 'she has never been officially concerned with foreign affairs . . . This Foreword therefore owes nothing to any official suggestion.' It seems odd to have included this statement unless she was anxious to protect herself against the imputation that she was merely serving as a mouthpiece for the Foreign Office. A comparison of the Foreign Office Memorandum with her pamphlet clearly establishes two things. First, the translations are entirely different, so that whatever use she may have made of the Memorandum, she definitely retranslated the passages. Second, there is a remarkable overlap between the two, amounting to about 70%, and although extracts vary considerably in length, the impression is that she supplemented her selections with some from the Memorandum.

Upon publication of her pamphlet, the Duchess provided Rennie Smith with literally hundreds of names and addresses of those who were to receive complimentary copies. The list included not only political, business, and professional leaders throughout the United Kingdom but also similarly placed comparable individuals throughout the British Commonwealth. The size of the first printing of Pamphlet no. 38 is unknown, but it was probably 10,000 copies, and within two months Smith was preparing to order another 10,000. On the whole, both public and private reactions were positive, and what criticism there was came from those regarded as cranks or known appeasers.

However, one critic in particular provoked the Duchess's grave concern. Dr A. P. Laurie, the former Principal of an Edinburgh technical college and a supposed anti-Nazi, compared extracts from the pamphlet with passages from the German edition of *Mein Kampf* and declared the former to be 'grossly inaccurate', claiming that they were lifted out of context and therefore made Hitler appear overly aggressive. He called for an investigation concerning the Friends of Europe, raising questions regarding the origin, membership, and financial backing of the group.

The Duchess reacted to Laurie's criticism by asking Rennie Smith to stop reissuing the pamphlet until she was able to check the allegations with an outside and impartial translator. She speculated that a revised German edition of *Mein Kampf* had come out, thus accounting for the discrepancies, yet she knew that Laurie was a 'cantankerous man . . . very uncompromising in his views', and that it might be dangerous to ignore his threats to publish a refutation of her pamphlet. Rennie Smith assured her that the utmost care had been taken with the original translation, and so it became primarily an exercise in convincing outsiders of its integrity in addition to seeking further prestigious endorsement of the Friends of Europe. In this endeavour she sought the advice and support of two of the most distinguished academics in Britain, Sir Charles Grant Robertson of Birmingham University and Sir Bernard Pares of London University. She also asked the Foreign Office to assist in verifying the quotations as well as clearing up the mystery of a possible revised German edition.

Ralph Wigram, who had taken such an interest in her project earlier in the year, was first to reply. He said the Foreign Office's official translator had reviewed the translation and, while noting a number of possible minor stylistic changes, had nothing substantive to suggest. Wigram was also able to put her at ease about a revised version, as the British Embassy in Berlin ascertained definitely that no changes had been made in the 1936 edition. However, he begged her not to refer to the Foreign Office as the source of this information. Nothing came of the Laurie affair, but it gave the Duchess and the Friends of Europe an opportunity to make a few changes and corrections in the pamphlet before printing another 10,000 copies. Reprints continued to sell briskly right up to the outbreak of war in 1939.[18]

As previously noted, the Duchess of Atholl's pamphlet did include some extracts which were not part of the Foreign Office Memorandum prepared in Berlin in 1936. It is instructive to see what she thought worth adding to her compilation. In *Mein Kampf*, Hitler stressed Germany's determination to recover territory lost after the First World War:

Let us make up our minds that we shall never win back the lost territory by solemn invocation of the Lord, or by pious hopes based on the League of Nations, but only by force of arms . . . Today, I am led by the sober consideration that lost territories are not won back by the volubility of Parliamentary gas-bags, but must be won by sharpened word, that is, by bloody struggle.

More than to recover former lands, Hitler called for Germany to expand and to pursue the dream of Pan-Germanism:

German Austria must return again to the great German Father land; this not for any kind of economic considerations. No, even if this union from an economic point of view were of no import-ance, or even if it were injurious, yet it must take place. The same blood belongs to a single Empire. The German people possesses no moral right to colonial activity so long as it is not able to unite its own sons in a common State. Only when the boundaries of the Reich include even the last German . . . does there arise from the need of its own people the moral right to acquire foreign soil. The plough then gives place to the sword and out of the tears of war springs daily bread for posterity.

The theme of *Lebensraum* again crops us, especially directed toward the East:

We start anew where we terminated six Centuries ago. We reverse the eternal Germanic migration to the South and to the West of Europe and look Eastwards. In this way we bring to an end the colonial and trade policies of pre-war times and pass over to the territorial policy of the future.

If we speak of new soil we can but think first of Russia and her subject border states.

The Friends of Europe pamphlet especially underscored the passages in *Mein Kampf* referring to France:

There must be full clarity about one thing. The deadly enemy of the German people now is and forever will be, France. It does not matter who rules in France, whether Bourbons or Jacobins, Bonapartists or bourgeois democrats, clerical republicans or red Bolshevists. The ultimate aim of French foreign policy will always be the attempt to seize the Rhine frontier and to secure through the crushing and dismemberment of Germany the possession of this river.

Every Power is our natural ally which finds French domination of the Continent insupportable. No road to such a Power must seem too difficult for us and no sacrifice too great if it only provides the final result of the possibility of overthrowing our grimmest hater, France. Our smaller wounds we can leave to the healing influence of time, provided we find a way completely to be rid of the greatest.

Hitler's decision to seek an alliance with Russia in August 1939 is prefigured by one of the pamphlet's quotations:

Let it not be said that one need not think at once of war in case of an alliance with Russia, or if so, that one would be able to make thorough preparations for such war. No. An alliance whose purpose does not comprise the intention to make war is senseless and worthless. Alliances are made only for fighting. And though the considerations underlying an Alliance may be far ahead in the future, it is nevertheless the prospect of military development which determines the course. Get rid of the idea that any Power enters into an Alliance without such an objective.

Finally, we have Hitler's description of the Big Lie:

One acted on the very correct principle that the size of the lie is a definite factor in causing it to be believed, for the vast masses of the nation are in the depths of their hearts more easily deceived than they are consciously and intentionally bad. The primitive simplicity of their minds renders them a more easy prey to a big lie than a small one, for they themselves often tell little lies but would be ashamed to tell big ones. Such a form of lying would never enter their heads. They would never credit to others the possibility of such great impudence as the complete reversal of facts by others. Even explanations would long leave them in doubt and hesitation and any trifling reason would dispose them to accept the thing as true. Something therefore always remains and sticks from the most impudent lies, a fact which all bodies and individuals concerned in the art of lying in this world know only too well, and hence they stop at nothing to achieve this end.

The justification for providing the British public with such quotations from *Mein Kampf* came from a sense of moral outrage and fear felt by those who were conscious of the discrepancies between the full German text and the Dugdale translation. In her Foreword, the Duchess condemned the abridged *My Struggle* because it:

effectively bars the way to the publication of a faithful English translation. *My Struggle* contains none of the passages which most clearly reveal Herr Hitler's policy, or, if it attempts to reproduce them, it does so in most cases in a form so mutilated or mistranslated as to leave in them little or nothing of their original meaning . . . No one, therefore, who reads *My Struggle* can have any idea of the foreign policy set forth in the original.

By the spring of 1936 the Foreign Office and the Duchess of Atholl both felt that the public in general, and the Cabinet in particular, should be alerted to Hitler's foreign policy aims. In March Hitler had ordered the military occupation of the Rhineland in flagrant violation of the Versailles Treaty, and for the first time since coming to power, he had made an overtly aggressive move rather than a series of defensive measures aimed at rearmament and restoration. A fuller understanding of Hitler's foreign policy statements seemed essential if the European powers were to anticipate his future moves. Domestic policy studied in the light of his auto-biography was one thing, but it was quite another to be forced into playing a sinister diplomatic parlour game of guessing where he would strike next.

In order to penetrate the philosophy of *Mein Kampf* more deeply, Ralph Wigram asked the distinguished Oxford historian, E. L. Woodward, to compose a letter on the subject. Woodward obliged, saying that there was little or nothing new in Hitler's ideas, but that they were ominous nevertheless.

Because of her Prussian heritage, Germany was especially attracted to militarism, and even anti-semitism had Germanic roots. In June 1936 Wigram wrote the following Foreign Office Minute:

Ignorant people here are very fond of saying that when he wrote 'Mein Kampf' Hitler was an unknown person in opposition and indeed in prison; and that, therefore, no more attention should be paid to the ideas in 'Mein Kampf' than would be paid, for instance, to a speech by Mr. Lloyd George in opposition.

Mr. Woodward's letter destroys this theory which could only be held by people who are completely ignorant of Germany and the history of the philosophy of Prussia.

If anyone is interested in the matter, I can give them a note containing a number of extracts which I have made recently from Clausewitz 'On War'; they will be surprised to see how the teaching given in one of the creators of the modern Prussian general staff fits in with some of the ideas of 'Mein Kampf'.

About a month later Anthony Eden commented: 'This is so interesting that I feel tempted to circulate it to my colleagues [in the Cabinet] or to some of them. Would there be any objection?'[19] Before agreeing to Eden's request, Wigram thought he should ask Woodward to revise his letter, since it had been hastily drafted in the first place. The great interest in Woodward's letter attests again the Foreign Office's desire to both understand and exploit the autobiography of Germany's head of state.

Divining Hitler's intentions became even more urgent following the fall of Austria in 1938 and German acquisition of the Sudetenland in the autumn of that year. On 6 December, Sir George Ogilvie-Forbes wrote to the Foreign Secretary, Lord Halifax, from Berlin:[20]

Chapter xiv of 'Mein Kampf' defines in some detail Herr Hitler's policy of eastern expansion. Germany, he declares, cannot be a world Power, however strong she may be militarily, unless she

42

increases her territory. 'If the National Socialist movement is to be consecrated before history to fulfil a great mission for our people, it must, permeated by the recognition of, and filled with sorrow for, the nation's real position on this earth, boldly and deliberately take up the battle against the aimlessness and incapacity which have hitherto led our German people on the road of its foreign policy. It must, without regard to "tradition" and prejudice, find the courage to assemble our people and its strength for the advance on that road which leads from the present narrowness of this people's territory to new ground and land, thus freeing it for ever from the danger of perishing on this earth or having to serve other nations as a helot people . . . The right to land and territory can become a duty if without an extension of territory a great people appears doomed to go down, particularly if it is not a question of some little nigger people, but of the Germanic Mother of Life, which has given the present-day world its cultural aspect. Germany will be either a world Power or nothing . . . Therefore, we National Socialists deliberately draw a line under the foreign policy of the pre-war period. We start where we finished 600 years ago. We stop the eternal Germanic drive to the south and west of Europe and turn our eyes to the land in the east . . . When to-day we talk of new land and territory in Europe, we can only think in the first place of Russia and her vassal border States.'

2. There have hitherto been two distinct stages in the attainment of German aims. The first was concerned with the removal of the servitudes of the peace treaties within the boundaries of the post-war Reich. During this period we saw the rearmament of Germany and the reoccupation of the Rhineland. This achievement, as Herr Hitler foretold in 'Mein Kampf', made Germany a desirable ally ('bündnisfähig') and the connexion with Italy was formed. The consequent accession of strength enabled Herr Hitler to embark on the second stage, namely, the union of all Germans in 'Grossdeutschland'. It is true that certain German pockets still remain outside the Reich, but these are considered so insignificant and their eventual incorporation so easy that they need not be considered.

3. It is the general conviction in Germany to-day that Herr Hitler is now about to embark on the third stage of his programme,

namely, expansion beyond the boundaries of the territories inhabited by Germans. How exactly this is to be achieved is the subject of much speculation. One thing is certain: Nazi aims are on a grandiose scale, and there is no limit to their ultimate ambitions. There seems to be a consensus of opinion in both Nazi and non-Nazi circles that the next objective, which may even be undertaken in 1939, is the establishment, with or without Polish co-operation, of an independent Russian Ukraine under German tutelage. This operation might conceivably be formed by peaceful means owing to the inability of Russia to resist, but it is assumed that war will be necessary. The question as to whether the Western Powers would remain neutral in the event of German aggression on Russia is being canvassed, but it appears to be thought by most people that neither France nor England would be prepared to march in the defence of the integrity of Russia, or of Ukrainian independence of Russia. The virtual possession of the Ukraine with all its resources, together with German hegemony in the Balkans and an outlet in the Mediterranean via Italy, would, it is claimed, render Germany completely proof against blockade. It would at the same time extend the area in which the German economic system is operating, and so relieve anxiety as to the economic future of this country.

4. There is a school of thought here which believes that Herr Hitler will not risk a Russian adventure until he has made quite certain that his western flank will not be attacked while he is operating in the east, and that consequently his first task will be to liquidate France and England, before British rearmament is ready. This aim could be approached in two ways: either by starting a war of aggression on both France and England, using Italian claims against France as a pretext, or by assuring that France would be neutral and concentrating on England . . .

5. Another section of opinion here believes that Herr Hitler will in the immediate future feel debarred by the assurance given in his Sportpalast speech of September 26 from any act of territorial aggression, and that he will concentrate on internal problems, whilst extending German influence in the Balkans by peaceful means, if that epithet may be applied to German methods. The majority of Germans, however, reject this relatively comfortable

theory on the ground that Herr Hitler is anxious to make his next move before British rearmament is further advanced.

6. I learn from an official source, which I believe to be reliable and which did not attempt to deny that the Chancellor was brewing trouble, that Herr Hitler had as yet not made up his mind; in other words, the tiger was in his lair waiting to see which way to spring. It is indeed the profound conviction of almost every thinking German that the tiger will spring and very soon. It is known that he is regretting not having taken a stronger line in September, and is abusing his moderate counsellors for their pusillanimity . .

This dispatch helped to inspire Sir Alexander Cadogan, the Permanent Under-Secretary of the Foreign Office, to prepare a paper entitled 'Possibility of a German attack on the East'. In his diary for 17 January 1939 he recorded:[21]

We cannot know whether Hitler will decide to go East, remaining on the defensive in the West, or whether he will deal with the West first, so as to gain a free hand in Eastern Europe. It would seem more logical (and more in accordance with *Mein Kampf*) that he should first acquire control over the resources of Eastern and South-Eastern Europe, and then, thus reinforced, turn against the West.

Here we have a classic example of how difficult it was to use *Mein Kampf* as a guide to future German action. From what Hitler had written back in 1925–6, one could just as easily have drawn the opposite conclusion from Cadogan's. In any case, it is clear that the Foreign Office took full cognizance of *Mein Kampf* and tried to glean Hitler's intentions from its pages.

Can the same be said of Prime Minister Neville Chamberlain and those who were his closest advisers? Many people at the time and since have been convinced that Chamberlain was either ignorant of the contents of *Mein Kampf* or failed to profit from an exposure to it. Typical was a comment in the American magazine, *Forum*, in May 1939: 'It is said that Mr. Chamberlain never got round to reading *Mein Kampf*.

It is a pity that some secretary did not make a *précis* of it for him.'[22] Sir John W. Wheeler-Bennett, the historian, later wrote concerning the Munich crisis: 'Mr. Chamberlain, it should be stated, had not at this moment read *Mein Kampf*, of which only an abridged edition existed in English. It was not until after his return from Munich that he requested the Foreign Office to prepare and translate suitable extracts for his perusal.'[23] Chamberlain's most vociferous critic has been the historian, A. L. Rowse, who, when speaking of the Prime Minister and his close advisers, lamented: 'Not one of these men in high place in those years ever so much as read *Mein Kampf*, or would listen to anybody who had. They really did not know what they were dealing with, or the nature and degree of the evil thing they were up against.'[24]

For years Chamberlain has been criticized by historians for ignoring the advice of professional diplomats and foreign policy experts while favouring 'amateurs' like Sir Horace Wilson, his industrial adviser; Geoffrey Dawson of *The Times*; Lord Lothian, editor and civil servant; and Thomas Jones, the former Assistant Secretary to the Cabinet. As one biographer noted: 'Chamberlain's papers in this as in earlier periods show his respect and regard for Eden, though not for the Foreign Office.'[25]

Chamberlain and his confidants were in general agreement that the most obnoxious Foreign Office expert was Sir Robert (later Lord) Vansittart. Even Eden tired of Vansittart's gloomy prognostications and seeming inefficiency, and so replaced him as Permanent Under-Secretary of State by Alexander Cadogan. The Foreign Office lost another strong voice against appeasement with the death of Ralph Wigram in 1936. Then in February 1938 Eden resigned, and was re-placed by the initially more complacent Viscount Halifax. Only after the Munich crisis did the new Foreign Secretary become thoroughly convinced of the need to curb further Nazi aggression.

The British Foreign Office and *Mein Kampf*

According to Rowse, the appeasers were poorly prepared to grapple with Hitler and the Nazis because they had studied only the classics rather than modern history and modern languages:[26]

T.J. [Tom Jones] knew not a word of German, any more than Lothian did; neither of them had any more knowledge of Germany, German history or what Germans were like, than Baldwin or Chamberlain had. Yet they all conspired to undermine and in the end get rid of Vansittart in the Foreign Office, who had a life-long acquaintance with all these matters . . .

On the other hand, historians like Christopher Thorne have been sympathetic with the attitudes of the so-called appeasers:[27]

To 'appease' was to settle just grievances, not to cringe and betray. . . . Such idealist overtones were a particularly British feature of appeasement, and are prominent when one examines the arguments of the smaller circle of 'appeasers' in or near the seats of power . . . [They] were seeking not so much to build the most powerful coalition possible as to reaffirm the 'moral basis' of British foreign policy – the rights of smaller states, the sanctity of international obligations, the repudiation of threats and force.

Still others, such as Chamberlain's biographer, Keith Feiling, contend that the Prime Minister was well informed about the situation in Germany, citing the fact that when Stephen H. Roberts published *The House That Hitler Built* in 1938, Chamberlain read and admired it, although he questioned some of its conclusions.[28] The most recent scholar preparing a full-scale biography of Chamberlain is David N. Dilks. We asked him whether he thought that Chamberlain had ever read *Mein Kampf*, and, if so, what difference it had made. He replied:[30]

It isn't true that Chamberlain did not read *Mein Kampf*. Like other members of the Cabinet, he read copious extracts from *Mein Kampf* circulated with a commentary by the Foreign Secretary, Mr. Eden, in 1936. Chamberlain may very well have read the expurgated version of *Mein Kampf* before that, and certainly was familiar from the circulated reports of thc Embassy at Berlin with the main outline of the creed of National Socialism, in so far as it had one. When the unexpurgated edition of *Mein Kampf* at last became available in English, Chamberlain at once bought his own copy and annotated portions of it. That copy is still in the hands of his family and I have seen it.

In other words, there is not in my judgment any reason to believe that British policy derived from ignorance on Chamberlain's part, or that of anyone else, of *Mein Kampf*. Whether it was correctly interpreted, or whether indeed it was possible to interpret correctly, is another question.

In many respects, D. C. Watt agrees with Dilks on the broader issues of appeasement:[30]

It is now apparent that within the Foreign Office, the three armed services, the Civil Service and the Cabinet, there were few illusions at any time about the nature of the threat to the peace constituted by Hitler. From the reports of the Defence Requirements sub-committee of 1933–34, from the exhortations of Lord Vansittart, from the increasing knowledge we now have of Chamberlain's private views, it is clear that the idea that there was any blindness to the peril or desire to divert it on other targets, against the Soviet Union for example, a view still maintained in some circles, is quite mistaken. It is rather that those responsible for the ultimate decisions could not be convinced of the unavoidable nature of the coming conflict with Nazi Germany. They could see a threat but not its certainty . . . They listened to the voices within their own circles who maintained an alternative view: that a policy of judicious and controlled concession, designed to remove the grievances and injustices on which Nazi chauvinism throve, would draw its teeth and make it tolerable as a neighbour on the European Continent.

Indeed Chamberlain espoused such an 'alternative view',

and judged that the Treaty of Versailles had been too harsh, the reparations debt unduly high, and Woodrow Wilson's principle of Self-Determination openly flouted. Years later, Vansittart sardonically dismissed these arguments out of hand. 'The world swallowed the Reparations swindle just as it swallowed the Bowdlerised version of *Mein Kampf* – another impudent and highly successful fraud.'[31]

Over the years the historiographical literature and debate on British foreign policy in the 1930s have assumed monumental proportions. Here it has only been possible to touch upon a few major characteristics of that controversial decade as viewed through the prism of *Mein Kampf*. Nevertheless, a few conclusions emerge from the foregoing evidence. From 1933 on, it seems clear that the Foreign Office was reasonably well informed about the contents of Hitler's autobiography, and sought on several occasions to make some use of it. Two Foreign Secretaries – Sir John Simon in 1933 and Anthony Eden in 1936 – took the trouble to circulate summaries of Hitler's book to members of the Cabinet. At the same time, there is no firm evidence that either Stanley Baldwin or Neville Chamberlain ever read the Dugdale abridgment. By contrast it is interesting to note Franklin D. Roosevelt's comment inside his personal copy of the Dugdale translation: 'The White House – 1933 – This translation is so expurgated as to give a wholly false view of what Hitler is and says – the German original would make a different story.'[32]

Following the Munich crisis of September 1938, Chamberlain and the appeasers hoped against hope that Hitler would be content with what he had achieved and would not precipitate a general war. Having occupied the Rhineland and having rapidly rearmed, Germany was clearly a major power on the Continent. Austria had been incorporated into the new Reich, and the Sudeten Germans had been reunited with the Fatherland. More than most countries, Germany had recovered from the Depression. Yet Munich augmented

British fears by bringing Europe to the brink of war. As General Ironside noted at the time:[33]

Chamberlain is of course right . . . We have not the means of defending ourselves and he knows it . . . We cannot expose ourselves now to a German attack. We simply commit suicide if we do.

Britain was left wondering whether, if Hitler was still bent on aggression, he would move first toward the East or the West. Foreign Office officials like Cadogan pondered this question again and again in early 1939. Unfortunately, on such a point *Mein Kampf* was thoroughly ambiguous. It might provide a fairly reliable insight into Hitler's ultimate goals, it might even contain Hitler's entire *Weltanschauung*, but it was an extraordinarily opaque lens for perceiving Hitler's next tactical move. In retrospect it usually made sense; in prospect it deceived as often as it revealed.

III

James Murphy and the 1939 unabridged London edition

Although an English-language abridgment of *Mein Kampf* first appeared in October 1933, a full translation was not issued until early 1939. Then, in February of that year, two competing versions appeared in the United States, followed a month later by one published in London. The latter was translated by Dr James Murphy and brought out by Hurst & Blackett, a subsidiary of the Hutchinson Publishing Group Ltd, who had published Dugdale's abridged translation. Heretofore Murphy's translation has received scant attention, and many questions surrounding it remain unanswered.[1]

During the 1930s it was generally assumed, officially and unofficially, that Hitler would not authorize a full translation of his autobiography. As late as February 1939, the head of the Central Department of the Foreign Office, William Strang, wrote, 'as regards the publication of Hitler's "Mein Kampf" or any portion of it, the difficulty is that Hitler himself owns the copyright and has hitherto declined to allow full translations to be published abroad'. If that, indeed, was the case, how did three separate and unabridged English-language editions make their appearance within the next six weeks? Had the Nazis relented, or were the translations published without authorization? Few reviewers in 1939 noticed this paradox. R. C. K. Ensor of the *Spectator* remarked simply, 'of the circumstances, in which the mask has now been withdrawn, we are unaware'.[2] A later commentator mentioned that the translator of the London edition, James Murphy, was 'an official translator in Dr. Goebbels' Ministry of Propaganda',[3] but if this were so, why did Hurst & Blackett choose his version? Were there any significant differences between the American and English editions? And finally, who was James Murphy? Standard biographical references do not list him, nor do the surviving records of the Hutchinson Publishing Group Ltd.

Fortunately is it now possible to answer most of these uncertainties, thanks to the exceedingly kind cooperation of Mrs Mary Murphy, widow of the translator. A few of the surviving German records also throw light on the subject, while valuable insight comes from discussion and correspondence with a few key individuals still living in Great Britain.[4]

James Murphy (1880–1946) was born and educated in Ireland.[5] Prior to the First World War he travelled extensively on the Continent and in the United States, but during the war he remained in Britain, combining freelance journalism with managing the Italian information office in London. One of his responsibilities in this connection was to edit a weekly periodical, *Modern Italy*, which sought to influence the deliberations at the Paris Peace Conference. This led to his return to Rome in 1922 where he was occupied with writing articles about Italy for various British newspapers. In 1925 the Italian government made it abundantly clear that his anti-Fascist attitudes were unappreciated, and that it would be well for him to leave. The next few years he spent in Paris, where he continued to write for British and American periodicals, primarily concerning Italian affairs.

A suggestion by a friend, urging him to combine his knowledge of Europe with his talent for public speaking, induced him to undertake a lecture tour of America. He arrived in New York City in the autumn of 1927, and before long managed to convert a six-month ramble into an elaborate two-year lecture circuit including universities, women's clubs, and town hall forums.

1930–2 found him back in Berlin editing yet another new periodical, *International Forum*. Only four issues of this extraordinary monthly were published, but in its brief life it counted among its contributors such luminaries as Thomas Mann, Max Planck, Arnold Zweig, Erwin Schrödinger, Ernst Simmel, Werner Sombart, and John Galsworthy. Because the magazine already necessitated so much translating, Murphy decided to try some larger translations as well. During the decade he thus completed half a dozen major works, including Planck's *Where is Science Going?* and Schrödinger's *Science and the Human Temperament*.

The severity of the Depression made it especially hard for foreigners to make a living in Germany, and so Murphy was forced to return to Great Britain in 1932. Feeling that his experience of living in Germany would provide considerable insight into how and why the Nazis came to power, he began to work on a book about Adolf Hitler in which he tried to explain why so many Germans were attracted to the Nazi cause. *Adolf Hitler: the Drama of His Career* (London: Chapman & Hall) appeared in the spring of 1934. The Nazis were not slow to take notice, as they were always on the look-out for foreigners who were sympathetic to their movement, or at least not overtly hostile. So they offered Murphy a job, and he was soon back in Berlin, but this time it was a very different Berlin from the one he had known just two years before. Serving as the official translator of Hitler's speeches in a sub-department of the Ministry of Public Enlightenment and Propaganda, he was impressed with Hitler's revitalization of the country despite the obvious crudities and sinister implications of the regime. His acquaintances were mostly Germans, many of whom had emigrated, but who were induced to return in the interest of rebuilding a greater Germany.

53

Hitler's *Mein Kampf* in Britain and America

On his return to Germany in 1934 he openly ridiculed the Nazis for their clumsy phrases and makeshift translations of major policy statements as well as their utter lack of familiarity with overseas audiences. The English-language abridgment of *Mein Kampf* came in for special scorn. It was a badly garbled version, he contended, and if foreigners were ever to understand Hitler's ideas and aspirations, they must have access to a fluent and idiomatic translation of the full text. The German Ambassador to the United States, Hans Dieckhoff, made much the same point. To his superiors in Berlin he wrote:[6]

Judging by the interest that the American public increasingly shows towards the Führer's book, I would consider it extremely desirable if such an edition could appear in America. The abridged edition is thought to be unauthoritative and alleged quotations from 'Mein Kampf' which are obviously false cannot be refuted because the necessary documentary proof is missing.

Faced with sentiments such as these, it is no wonder that the Nazis gave serious thought to issuing *Mein Kampf* in its entirety. Toward the end of 1936 the Propaganda Ministry ordered Murphy to begin work on a complete translation. The clear implication was that his version would be officially sanctioned for release abroad. However, six months later, without Murphy's knowledge, a mysterious backing-down occurred. A spokesman for the Propaganda Ministry quietly announced to his counterpart in the Foreign Ministry: 'there are for the moment some fundamental difficulties, so that there is no chance of its being published in the near future'.[7]

In the months that followed, periodic inquiries were made concerning a complete English or American edition, but the response was always vague. Nevertheless, with the help of a talented German woman who became his assistant, Murphy finished his translation by the autumn of 1937. Fräulein Greta Lorcke was German by birth. She had studied English in the

United States and could speak and write it fluently. When Murphy first met her in Berlin in 1936, he had been struck by her exceptional intelligence, which far outdistanced that of an average secretary or editorial assistant.

What he did not learn until years later was that she and her husband-to-be, Adam Kuckoff, were members of the notorious Soviet spy ring, the *Rote Kapelle*. In 1936, Greta Lorcke was trying to live as inconspicuously as possible in Berlin, keeping her eyes and ears open, and making periodic reports to her superiors. Her becoming an assistant of Murphy's provided a convenient cover for her while being at the same time ideologically rewarding.

In her recently published memoirs,[8] Frau Kuckoff describes her first meeting with Murphy, admitting that she knew something of his background beforehand. She was introduced to him by the author, Otto Zoff, whose flat the Murphys rented while Zoff was in Italy:

I knew that Mr. M. had translated Planck into English. He had the reputation of converting dry prose into something splendid by virtue of his unusually rich and beautiful gift for language . . . I was very much impressed by him as he came to meet me in the main lobby. He was a handsome man – two metres tall and carried his one hundred kilos with a regal dignity – a man who inspired confidence. The way he discussed his translation work, with which I was to assist him, made me believe that he was no friend of National Socialism. How else could Otto Zoff have recommended me to him? Yet how could such a person do this sort of work when he did not subscribe to the official Party goal of propagating National Socialist ideas? This was something I hoped to discover.

After some months of helping Murphy translate articles and speeches, she was presented with a disturbing challenge:

Then came M.'s offer to help him with the translation of Hitler's *Mein Kampf* into English . . . To be sure, I had previously heard of an abridged translation, but how could the Western nations recognize the great danger facing them, if they could not learn of Hitler's intentions from his own writings or were misinformed about them? Somehow I had to convince Arvid Harnack.

Harnack was her superior in the Berlin spy ring, and he found it difficult to believe that there was nothing already published that adequately revealed Hitler's plans to the English-speaking world. She urged her involvement in the project on the grounds that ' "no-one will forgive us if we fail to make the truth accessible" '.

By the beginning of 1937 the task of translating *Mein Kampf* was well under way:

What Mr. M. prepared and showed to me was of such excellent quality that one could hardly detect the vulgarity of the original. Mr. M. was not only well versed in science but also in history, and there was scarcely a major literary work which his phenomenal memory could not quote. However, all this contributed to a bad cause. I tried to convince him that the work would lose its original character, with its mass appeal, if he imposed too much of his own erudition. I wanted the book to retain its shameless stirring up of the masses. My protests were not always effective.

Recently, in a private letter to us she echoed the same concern.

As I wrote in my book, he was much too conscientious in his work not to employ his greatest skill when using the English language. He must have known that I altered his wonderful translation whenever I had the chance, even though he disagreed with such changes.

However, their great effort was soon thwarted by the Propaganda Ministry, which sequestered all the completed copies of the manuscript. Before long, political and military events began to dominate people's lives. In rapid succession two of Hitler's chief military advisers, von Blomberg and von Fritsch, were dismissed; Foreign Minister von Neurath was replaced by the Nazi Party faithful, von Ribbentrop;

and Germany invaded Austria in March 1938. By this time too, Murphy's own position had altered considerably. As an official German memorandum phrased it, Murphy was dismissed from the Propaganda Ministry because of his general 'unreliability'. Although a few semi-official translation jobs still came his way, after this, his standing with the government was badly undermined. Not only did he increasingly deride the policies of Mussolini and Hitler, but once he even refused to translate a portion of one of Hitler's speeches which was directed against Anthony Eden, and which to Murphy was patently absurd. The tension during those months was later described by Murphy's wife:[9]

I knew he would not be further employed. I feared we might starve. I feared there would be war and as we all had Irish Free State passports we could have stayed on in Berlin. Perhaps James would not move in time. Terrified of the future, I began to give English lessons and was surprised to find that all my pupils were Jews. I heard very strange stories from them. Then I got more frightened and begged James to let me and the children return to England. He did, and we came to my mother. We travelled from Hamburg with just ten marks each (all that was allowed out of the country in those years) and I think I had two pound notes hidden in the foot of my stocking.

Mary Murphy and her two children reached Southampton on 10 June 1938 via the American cargo vessel, *President Roosevelt*, too poor to be able to tip any of the ship's crew. For the next six months they were particularly hard-pressed financially, and it was this predicament which, in large measure, induced James to seek a publisher for his translation of *Mein Kampf*. During that summer he hastily completed the miscellaneous translations previously commissioned, and sailed for England in early September, leaving behind his furniture and personal possessions in Berlin in case he eventually decided to return there.

In London he immediately went to seek the advice of his

literary agent, Robert Sommerville, as to the best way of finding a publisher for his translation of *Mein Kampf.* 1938 found everybody preoccupied with the growing crisis in Czechoslovakia, and this fostered great interest in what Hitler had written in *Mein Kampf* about his ultimate aims. Following the Munich Agreement Murphy approached one of the leading London publishers, and, as Mary Murphy recorded in her diary:

He is very optimistic [about] flying over to Berlin to try and arrange for the publication of MEIN KAMPF. Heinemann are mad to get it and offer very good money for it indeed.

However, Heinemann were reluctant to proceed until certain obvious obstacles were overcome. They knew what Murphy must not have realized prior to his return to England, namely, that the translation rights for *Mein Kampf* belonged exclusively to another London firm, Hurst & Blackett. A plausible case could be made out for regarding Hurst & Blackett's rights as extending only to the 1933 abridged edition, but Heinemann did not wish to risk an injunction, and urged Murphy to return to Berlin long enough to secure official authorization or proof that he had been commissioned by the German government. If this were done, then Heinemann were more than willing to go ahead with the venture.

Another and far more devastating complication was that Murphy had no personal copy of his translation. Could the Propaganda Ministry be persuaded to release it? To this end, he went along to the German Embassy in London and made preliminary inquiries. Meeting considerable resistance to his initial request, he resigned himself to returning to Berlin himself. Just before his departure, he stopped by the German Embassy to collect an entry visa. On the night he should have left for Germany, his wife was dismayed to find him back home again. As she later recalled:

He looked white and rather shaken . . . He told me he had gone

James Murphy and the 1939 London edition

to the German Embassy and while there someone had rung up
from Berlin and said: 'if Murphy is thinking of coming back to
Berlin, please tell him he is wasting his time'. Now, a few years
previously, James would not have taken the least notice of such a
warning, but by now his nerves were frayed. He had been working
under great duress for some time and perhaps deep down he had
his doubts about the rightness of what he was doing . . . Quite
desperate because of the lack of blankets and towels, I said: 'well,
if your agent will agree, I'll go. They won't notice me.' And his
agent agreed. My mother and a kind sister-in-law took charge of
the children, and I went in fear and trembling.

It took about ten days for Mary to make final preparations
for her departure. On Sunday, 6 November, she recorded in
her diary, 'This morning I left for Berlin. The crossing to
Ostend was good. I slept at Köln in the Kölnerhof Hotel.'
She was unable to make any appointments with officials in
the Propaganda Ministry until 10 November. The previous
night she witnessed the *Kristallnacht* destruction of Jewish
synagogues and private property throughout Germany:

At 1·00 o'clock this morning an organised onslaught started upon
all Jewish shops. Their windows were smashed, furniture hacked
to pieces in the streets, clothes burned. This took place in every big
town. Some of the Jews could only walk the streets and pass their
time in restaurants.

At the Propaganda Ministry she was ushered in to see
Heinrich Bohle, a former office colleague of James, of whom
she later said: 'Heini was an ignoramus and drove James
nearly mad.' The Murphys had always regarded Bohle as
utterly incompetent, holding on to his job solely on the
strength of his being the brother of Ernst Wilhelm Bohle,
head of the *Auslands-Organisation*. Of her meeting with him
she recorded:

I accomplished nothing. I asked to see the Hurst & Blackett
contract with the Eher Verlag [Hitler's publisher]; and for the

59

manuscript of MEIN KAMPF, or to obtain in writing an admission that James was authorised to translate MEIN KAMPF.

Failing to get anywhere with Bohle, she sought out another acquaintance in the Ministry:[10]

Talked to a little man I knew called Seyferth. He said: 'Mrs. Murphy, do you think I want to be put up against a wall and shot? I have a wife and two children.' I said: 'Of course you won't be shot, but you can't prevent MEIN KAMPF coming out in English because five Americans are working on it now, and you know at least that my husband's translation is an honest one and makes Hitler sound a sensible, reasonable human being. The others will not do a job like this.' But there was nothing doing. I had to go away from the Propaganda Department empty-handed. I had no money. My one-time housekeeper fed me.

One last chance remained. A former secretary of James' who had typed much of the translation still lived in Berlin. Mary decided to visit her that same Thursday evening, and, to her great relief, learned that a rough, hand-written draft had survived! On 20 November Mary left Berlin, having been unable to secure any kind of official authorization for a translation, but at least possessing the precious draft copy.

Now it was a race to see whether Murphy could persuade some publisher, in particular Hurst & Blackett, to issue the full text before a competing translation was commissioned or procured from America.

Meanwhile, Hurst & Blackett had one of its employees, William Kimber, sound out the German publishers about Murphy's role in the whole affair. A definitive response came from Eher Verlag:[11]

Today [21 November] we are able to inform you that Mr. Murphy has received no competent authorisation to dispose of the complete English edition in England. As you know there is a contract between our publishing house and you, and therefore if a complete translation of 'Mein Kampf' should ever appear, it could only do so through you. As we informed you in our last letter, there is for the moment no possibility of publishing the complete translation. You are still at liberty to publish the old edition, and if it becomes possible to issue the whole work in England, we shall of course notify you.

By November 1938, therefore, the German firm of Eher Verlag and the various governmental ministries in Germany considered that they had made their position clear. Yet within a month, two American firms announced their intention to issue the full text. One of these firms, Reynal & Hitchcock of New York, was duly licensed to do so by Houghton Mifflin of Boston, the purchasers of the translation rights in 1933. The other, Stackpole Sons of Harrisburg, Pennsylvania, and New York City, specifically rejected Reynal & Hitchcock's licensing agreement on the grounds that Houghton Mifflin had never acquired a legally valid claim to the American market in the first place. Although the Boston firm threatened to seek an injunction against the Pennsylvania 'pirates', both publishers were prepared to go ahead, regardless of what the Germans said. Official news of their intentions reached Hurst & Blackett on 31 December 1938,[12] but for the moment they were prepared to do nothing. As William Kimber explained to Murphy:[13]

We are watching the American situation regarding 'Mein Kampf' very closely, though of course whatever the outcome, it little affects the practical aspects of our position because, as you know, English copyright law is vastly different from that in the U.S.A. and our copyright of 'Mein Kampf' is unquestionably secure and exclusive although we have published only an abridged version.

At about this same time, the German Embassy in Washington and the Consulate-General in New York were informing the Foreign Ministry in Berlin of the forthcoming American translations and urging prompt action on the part of Eher Verlag. Finally the Germans began to realize that they must

61

act. On 9 January 1939 Max Amann, head of the Nazi Party publishing house, urged the Foreign Ministry to protest against the unauthorized American editions through the usual diplomatic channels. On 4 February the Foreign Ministry was informed by telephone that the matter had been brought to the attention of the Reichskanzlei, and that within a few days Hitler's attention would be drawn to it. As was so often the case in Nazi Germany, no one individual or department wished to make a decision on its own, least of all Eher Verlag, and so the problem was shunted from one office to another pending an eventual decision by someone, possibly the Führer himself.[14]

Amidst all the confusion surrounding the publication of unabridged translations, one point was generally not recognized in either Great Britain, the United States, or Germany. There was, in fact, a basic difference in the wording of the contracts with Hurst & Blackett and Houghton Mifflin. In the former, Eher Verlag agreed to supply the London firm 'immediately with a competent English translation', and Hurst & Blackett contracted to 'use the said translation for their editions of the said work subject to the translation meeting with their approval'. In the minds of the Germans, this meant that Hurst & Blackett had the right to publish a *specific abridged version* and nothing more. By contrast, the contract with Houghton Mifflin, while assuming the use of the same abridgment, conveyed to the Boston firm the rights for any future edition of *Mein Kampf* in America. The operative clause in the American contract read as follows, and we have italicized the key phrase:

1. The Proprietors hereby grant and assign to the Publishers the volume rights of a work the subject or title of which is MEIN KAMPF, by Adolf Hitler; together with any existing copyrights thereof, and with the exclusive right and power in their name or in the name of the Proprietors to take out copyright thereof in the United States; and to publish and sell said work in *editions, abridgments, and*

James Murphy and the 1939 London edition

selections during the term of any copyright and during any renewal, continuation, or extension thereof accruing to the Author, under the present or any future Act of Congress . . .

Thus, Houghton Mifflin and its licensee, Reynal & Hitchcock, felt wholly justified in issuing any portion of *Mein Kampf* whenever they chose, and they fully expected Eher Verlag to support them in their efforts to suppress the unauthorized Stackpole edition.

At this point the chronology of events is somewhat vague. Apparently sometime in January 1939 Hurst & Blackett determined to publish Murphy's translation, recognizing that the Americans were going ahead with their editions. Technically, the American versions could not legally be sold in Great Britain or its dependencies because of the way in which the translation rights were circumscribed by Eher Verlag. Walter Hutchinson, who made the decision to proceed, might well have assumed that the Houghton Mifflin contract was the same as that of his own firm of Hurst & Blackett, and if the Americans were prepared to risk a breach, so was he. Hutchinson also presumably knew that one of the reasons why the Germans refused permission had to do with anti-Nazi sentiments expressed in the introductions and notes to foreign editions. In fact, this was precisely what happened with the Reynal & Hitchcock version, where a committee of American scholars diligently augmented the text by a third with explanatory material. Hurst & Blackett may have conjectured that they would avoid Nazi retaliation if they published Murphy's translation with a minimum of annotation. The publishing records are silent on this point, but Murphy later stated that he had not wanted to write an introduction, and pressure from an unnamed quarter had been brought upon him to do so.[15] Whatever Hutchinson's reasons, it seems perfectly clear that he went ahead with Murphy's translation without securing any kind of authorization from Germany.

Hitler's *Mein Kampf* in Britain and America

Mrs Murphy recalls what then ensued:

... it was supposed to be completed in six weeks. We only had the rough, hand-written manuscript which I had brought over from Berlin in November 1938 ... I think we started at once, working in the bedroom where there was plenty of light, if little sun ... James bought two barrister's tables and there was the usual business of fitting up the room suitable to working ... MEIN KAMPF was finished after much anguish in February and I took a taxi early one morning to the printers at St. Albans with James's Translator's Note: the last finishing touch to the book.

The haste with which the volume was published was attested to by the trade journal, *The Bookseller*:

Hutchinson's moved almost as quickly as does Hitler himself. The text runs to 560 large pages of close print, yet it was set up in type in four working days. It was printed in three days. The translator, Mr. James Murphy, worked night and day during that period, sending proofs back in batches by taxi.

It appeared in London bookstalls on 20 March, three weeks after the publication of the two competing American editions.[16]

Reviews were mixed, though generally favourable to Murphy's rendering of the text. As a reviewer for *The Times* wrote: 'the translator has made an excellent job of 570 difficult pages, and his straightening out of the more involved sentences and jargon is masterly'. His introductory material fared less well, however. The *Spectator* and the *Daily Telegraph* commented respectively:[17]

Mr. Murphy, in a rather pro-Hitler Introduction, repeats the pro-Hitler plea, that *Mein Kampf* was written a good many years ago in conditions of special anti-French exasperation, and 'Hitler has declared that his acts and public speeches constitute a partial revision of his book.'

What, again, becomes of the argument that, as Chancellor Herr

James Murphy and the 1939 London edition

Hitler is not implicated by the programme of 'Mein Kampf' when we see every single item of that programme being fulfilled before our eyes with the most astonishing pertinacity.

Mrs Murphy remembers that 'by the time MEIN KAMPF came out in March the translator's preface cut no ice, because no soul in England had a wish to see anything from the German point of view'. It was, after all, during that same month that Hitler occupied the rest of Czechoslovakia.

Understandably most of the reviews were not concerned with the translation *per se*, but with the availability of the unexpurgated text. Some reviewers thought that the previous omissions were highly revealing, while others were unimpressed, feeling that the many gaps were merely haphazard. Few questioned why Hitler had relented and released the full text.

Just how different was Murphy's translation from others rendered at the time? Random sentences cannot be truly representative but they do highlight tendencies. As compared with two American translations published in 1939 and 1943,[18] Murphy more often used the past tense rather than Hitler's pluperfect, the active rather than the passive voice, and two shorter sentences where the original had been one long passage. Here are the opening sentences of chapter 2 as written first by Murphy, then by Reynal & Hitchcock's edition of 1939, and finally by Houghton Mifflin in 1943:

When my mother died my fate had already been decided in one respect. During the last months of her illness I went to Vienna to take the entrance examination for the Academy of Fine Arts. Armed with a bulky packet of sketches, I felt convinced that I should pass the examination quite easily. At the *Realschule* I was by far the best student in the drawing class, and since that time I had made more than ordinary progress in the practice of drawing. Therefore I was pleased with myself and was proud and happy at the prospect of what I considered an assured success.

Hitler's *Mein Kampf* in Britain and America

When my mother died, Fate had cast the die in one direction at least. During the last months of her suffering, I had gone to Vienna to take my entrance examination to the *Akademie*. I had set out with a lot of drawings, convinced that I would pass the examination with ease. At the *Realschule* I had been by far the best artist in my class; and since then my ability had improved greatly, so that my self-satisfaction made me hope both proudly and happily for the best.

When my mother died, Fate, at least in one respect, had made its decisions. In the last months of her sickness, I had gone to Vienna to take the entrance examination for the Academy. I had set out with a pile of drawings, convinced that it would be child's play to pass the examination. At the *Realschule* I had been by far the best in my class at drawing, and since then my ability had developed amazingly; my own satisfaction caused me to take a joyful pride in hoping for the best.

At the beginning of chapter 4 we notice two other characteristics: Murphy often inverted the word order, presumably in the interest of readability; and Houghton Mifflin, appearing last, occasionally borrowed phrases from either of the other two:

At last I came to Munich in the Spring of 1912. The city itself was as familiar to me as if I had lived for years within its walls. This was because my studies in architecture had been constantly turning my attention to the metropolis of German art.

In the spring of 1912 I came to Munich for good. The town itself was as familiar to me as if I had lived inside its walls for years. The reason for this was that my studies, step by step, directed me towards this metropolis of German art.

In the spring of 1912 I came at last to Munich. The city itself was as familiar to me as if I had lived for years within its walls. This is accounted for by my study which at every step had led me to this metropolis of German art.

James Murphy and the 1939 London edition

In chapter 5 Hitler speaks of the bourgeois climate that pervaded the years of his youth:

Individual countries increasingly assumed the appearance of commercial undertakings, grabbing territory and clients and concessions from each other under any and every kind of pretext. And it was all staged to an accompaniment of loud but innocuous shouting.

The individual States began more and more to resemble enterprises which cut the ground from under each other, stole each other's customers and orders, and tried to cheat each other by every means, setting this in a scene which was as noisy as it was harmless.

The various nations began to be more and more like private citizens who cut the ground from under one another's feet, stealing each other's customers and orders, trying in every way to get ahead of one another, and staging this whole act amid a hue and cry as loud as it is harmless.

Although Murphy's version was not invariably the tersest, it often gave the impression of greater conciseness and precision. In the following sentence which opens chapter 6, note Murphy's economy of words.

In watching the course of political events I was always struck by the active part which propaganda played in them.

At the time of my attentive following of all political events, the activities of propaganda had always been of extremely great interest to me.

Ever since I have been scrutinizing political events, I have taken a tremendous interest in propagandist activity.

Accurate sales figures for Murphy's translation are unfortunately not available. We do know that it went through many editions, including an elaborately illustrated one, and another put out in eighteen weekly parts. Robert Sommerville, Murphy's literary agent, reported that up until August

1939 about 32,000 copies had been sold. When war broke out in September, Hurst & Blackett were no longer obliged to deliver royalty statements to Eher Verlag, and this combined with the subsequent loss of Hutchinson's records from bombing, put a permanent seal on this information. It would not be at all surprising, however, if 150,000–200,000 copies were eventually sold.

The Murphys felt that they were never adequately remunerated for their work. No copy of the contract between Hurst & Blackett and James Murphy has ever turned up, but according to his fragmentary records, Murphy was paid an advance of £250, followed by an additional £150 six months later. Although this was a considerable sum for an average translation, Murphy hoped for a great deal more because the work had sold so well. For his part, Walter Hutchinson was reluctant to compensate Murphy too lavishly because of information contained in a letter he received from Germany just prior to its publication. Ironically, Hutchinson had to ask the Murphys to translate the letter into English, and in the absence of her husband, Mary was left with this chore. It turned out to be a savage attack on her husband, and, among other things, pointed out that he had already been well paid for his translation by the Propaganda Ministry. This being the case, Hutchinson shied away from reimbursing Murphy too generously for fear of alienating the German publishers and encouraging them to seek an injunction against Hurst & Blackett.[19]

Meanwhile, what was transpiring in Germany? Were the publishers and the government prepared to sit by while three separate and unabridged editions of *Mein Kampf* came out? Apparently not. However, as late as April 1939 ministers were still conferring with one another as to the best policy to pursue. Had German protests been rendered in late January or early February, they might have discouraged one or two of the translations, but by April all three translations had been released. In Berlin Consul Pownschab reviewed the whole situation in a lengthy memorandum,[20] reiterating that none of the three versions had secured official German sanction. Murphy's translations came in for special mention.

Apparently to keep up with the American publishing houses, the firm of Hurst & Blackett Ltd. of London also recently published its own unabridged edition of 'Mein Kampf'. Up to now Eher Verlag allowed them to sell only an abridged edition and expressly forbade an unabridged one. By comparing the text of the unauthorized edition with the manuscript of a certain Murphy, who was ordered by the Reich Minister of Public Enlightenment and Propaganda to produce an English version, it becomes clear that Mr. Murphy apparently took a copy of his work to London and sold it there.

Characterizing the contemporary state of affairs, Pownschab continued:

The Führer has refused to give his permission to publish an unabridged English translation of his work 'Mein Kampf'. This decision applies to Houghton Mifflin as well as to Hurst & Blackett, the two firms which had a contractual relationship with Eher Verlag. The Stackpole firm has neither the right to publish an abridged nor unabridged translation. The Führer wishes to avoid a newspaper campaign [against the British and American publishers] breaking out in the German press. Such a campaign has been proposed by Eher Verlag but the Führer has given orders to protest through diplomatic channels in Washington and London against the violation of the copyright of his work 'Mein Kampf' and to warn that there might be German retaliation if the unauthorized translations . . . should be allowed to continue.

On 24 April a conference of five officials from the Propaganda Ministry was called to discuss retaliatory steps that might be taken against Britain and the United States. Hans Dieckhoff, former and now discredited German Ambassador to Washington, sat in on the deliberations.

Meanwhile, German diplomats in New York, Boston and

Washington were urging their government to support Houghton Mifflin in its lawsuit against Stackpole. However, the German government did nothing, and this had the effect of tacitly supporting Hurst & Blackett in London and Houghton Mifflin in Boston. As far as one can determine, no formal diplomatic protests were ever lodged.

Twenty-five years later the London *Sunday Times* raised the same question and concluded:[21]

what isn't known is that the full pre-war edition was an unauthorised one. The original English edition was brought out in an abridged form in 1933. The publishing rights for this were fully and officially negotiated with Hitler's publishing representatives.

But it wasn't until six years later that a full unabridged version was published here. Mr. William Kimber, the publisher, who was then employed by Hutchinson's, says that the 1939 version was published 'in defiance of Hitler's wishes'.

William Kimber is probably the only person now living who was at that time close enough to Walter Hutchinson to know the criteria for decision-making, and unfortunately he declines to comment.

It now seems clear that the translations of February–March 1939 received no prior permission, but did acquire a kind of *de facto* approval. We surmise this first of all because Eher Verlag refused to challenge Houghton Mifflin's claim to copyright in the full American edition. Secondly, the Germans never brought any action against Hurst & Blackett. In fact, they did quite the opposite by inquiring about complimentary copies and royalty payments on the new and unabridged edition in the late spring of 1939. Hurst & Blackett's curt reply to Eher Verlag was: 'We would add that the new edition of "Mein Kampf" was not issued until this year, and therefore the particulars you require are not yet available', and their literary agent, Curtis Brown, added emphatically: 'we take the opportunity to emphasize that we have at no time been in contact with Dr. Murphy and that we are in no way responsible for the publishing of this translation by Hurst & Blackett'.[22]

Thus, by May 1939 the Germans had obviously come to terms with the existence of British and American translations even though they did not like what had happened. If war had not broken out in September, Hurst & Blackett would have rendered a routine statement of sales covering the first six months of the year on both the abridged and unabridged editions.

One is still left, nonetheless, with a paradox concerning Murphy's translation. Why did the Propaganda Ministry officially authorize it in 1936-7 only to refuse to release and publish it later? The presumption has always been that Hitler was trying to conceal his true motives and intentions from the outside world. However, by the late 1930s most of the provocative passages that had been omitted from the Dugdale abridgment had been widely published in a variety of newspaper articles, pamphlets such as those issued by the Friends of Europe, magazine articles, and innumerable critical books.

Hitler's actual motives may have been influenced by rather different concerns. If the full text were released in translation, could he insure that it would be free from hostile commentaries in introductions, forewords, and footnotes? The Nazi regime used this argument in successfully suppressing an unauthorized French translation in 1934. The edition in question had a preface by Marshal Lyautey which they considered offensive, and they won a favourable decision from the Commercial Court in Paris. All copies were seized and the type was broken up, with the further injunction that any bookseller who persisted in offering the work for sale would be heavily fined.[23]

The reason the German government failed to take prompt legal action in 1939 against 'unauthorized' editions was partly because Hurst & Blackett and Houghton Mifflin both had contracts for the abridgment which might have been construed (especially in the American case) to extend to unabridged editions. Then again, it may have been another instance of Hitler's well-known predilection to postpone decisions; and by the time he determined to act, it was too late to make an effective diplomatic protest.

IV

The American reaction to *Mein Kampf*, 1933–39

On 29 July 1933 Houghton Mifflin Company of Boston contracted with Hitler's publisher, Eher Verlag, to 'manufacture, publish, and offer said work for sale in book form'.[1] Houghton Mifflin were empowered to use the Dugdale abridged translation, thereby facilitating simultaneous Anglo-American publication in October. However, by the end of August, groups and individuals within the United States began to organize protests against the issuing of such an infamous work. One spokesman was quoted as saying: 'our efforts, through correspondence and editorial comments, having failed to impress upon Houghton Mifflin Company the perils of this vile book: "We charge the publishers with an attempt to cash in on the misery and catastrophe of an important section of the human family." '[2]

In September, a Wall Street broker, Louis Lober, joined with other New York City residents petitioning the Board of Education to discontinue purchasing textbooks from Houghton Mifflin on the grounds that: 'an American firm that knowingly lends its assistance in spreading the lying propaganda of a common gangster – propaganda that strikes at the very foundation of American institutions – should have no right to participate in the distribution of the tax-payers' money'.[3] Edward Mandel, Associate Superintendent of Education, rejoined:[4]

Hitler's *Mein Kampf* in Britain and America

The greatest service one can render humanity in general and Germany in particular is to place 'My Battle' within the reach of all, that each, for himself, may see whether the book is worthy or is an exhibition of ignorance, stupidity, and dullness. But neither ignorance nor stupidity nor dullness is a crime.

In its 'Annual Report for 1934', the American Jewish Committee acknowledged its efforts to counteract the publication of *My Battle*:[5]

When the publication of an English translation of Adolf Hitler's autobiography 'Mein Kampf' was announced, your Committee took steps to make the true nature of the book evident to the leaders of American public opinion. As part of its program in this direction, it issued in mimeograph form a translation of a number of passages from an original German edition, in which the author attacked not only the Jews but the liberal institutions that are at the basis of the government of the United States and in which he glorified war and the militaristic spirit. Because many of these selections were not included in the abridged English version issued in this country, your Committee felt it would be rendering a service to the American reading public by making it clear that the diluted and Bowdlerized version of the book as issued for American readers did not fully represent either the views or the temperament of its author. The list of quotations from the German edition of the autobiography was therefore sent to book reviewers throughout the country who were, in this manner, kept informed of the true nature of the book.

Private individuals also wrote to President Roosevelt, urging him to take action. Max Conn, head of a metals processing company in Chicago, wrote:[6]

It has come to my attention that Hitler's book, 'Mein Kampf', in English 'My Battle', which he has published in Germany for over five years, containing a lot of falsehoods about the Jewish people and being socialistic throughout the book, that this book ought not to be permitted to be published in our country.

Knowing your fair mindedness, both against the slandering of the Jews as well as against socialism and Nazi-ism, I wish you would be kind enough to issue instructions that the publishers, Houghton and Mifflin Co., Boston, Mass., is immediately informed to suppress the publication and if any books have already been sent to book dealers throughout the country, that they be recalled.

May I ask you, Mr. President, to be kind enough and give this matter prompt attention and let me hear from you on the subject.

A similar though more eloquent appeal was sent by the publisher of the *Chicago Israelite*:[7]

So, in conjunction with every Jew in the United States, I am agitated at a forthcoming publication of Hitler's scurrilities, 'My Battle' by Houghton Mifflin and Company of Boston, Mass. It is the utterance of venomous untruths about a large law-abiding peoples and I was wondering if there was not some way to stop the publication of this book.

It has stirred and inflamed prejudice and race-hatred to such an extent in Germany that a whole section of the people of that country have become Pariahs with a price upon each head. I am sure that this book will tend to cast contumely upon the Jews of America. No one would want to suppress the truth, but Hitler's vituperations against the Jews are the outpourings of a maddened zealot and has no place in America. It is simply Hitlerite propaganda against the Jews, Machiavellian in cunning.

Is there not some way that publication of this book can be suppressed?

These letters were turned over to the State Department and answered by J. P. Moffat, Chief of the Division for Western European Affairs:[8]

In reply I am under the necessity of inviting your attention to the provisions of the Constitution of the United States which guarantee freedom of speech and of the press. In the circumstances, it is not possible for this Government to take action of the nature which you suggest. If, however, a publication violates existing laws of libel or slander, interested persons may, of course, under these laws resort to court action.

For their part, Houghton Mifflin felt that they were being ill used in this public and private clamour. In a note accompanying a complimentary copy of *My Battle* to President Roosevelt, one of the Company's officers, Roger L. Scaife, set forth the Company's predicament:[9]

In confidence I may add that we have had no end of trouble over the book – protests from the Jews by the hundreds, and not all of them from the common run of shad. Such prominent citizens as Louis Kirstein and Samuel Untermeyer and others have added their protest, although I am glad to say that a number of intellectual Jews have also written complimenting us upon the stand we have taken.

A group of Jews in New York petitioned the New York Board of Education to refrain from the purchase of any of our books because we are issuing Herr Hitler's volume, but I am glad to report that the Board refused to consider the request, claiming that the freedom of our Press should be maintained. Other forms of restraint have been brought to our attention in no uncertain words.

I thought the incident worthy of your attention, especially in view of the number of public-spirited individuals from this race who hold important posts under your Administration.

At this time Louis Kirstein was President of Filene's, the major department store in Boston, and Samuel Untermeyer was an internationally known lawyer and leading proponent of civil rights. In the 1920s Untermeyer had successfully represented clients in a suit against Henry Ford for anti-semitic articles in both the *Dearborn Independent* and a volume entitled *The International Jew*. Subsequently Ford was ordered to make a formal retraction in the columns of his newspaper as well as to withdraw and destroy all copies of the offending book. Untermeyer was also a founder of the Anti-Nazi League to Champion Human Rights and a leader in the Jewish boycott of German goods in retaliation for Nazi boycotts and persecution. Thus, as far as one can judge, American Jewish reaction to the Dugdale abridgment of *Mein Kampf* was far more vehement than in Britain.

Book reviewers on both sides of the Atlantic tended to be far more judicious than these public protests. Typical of press comment was a review by John Chamberlain in the *New York Times* on the day of publication.[10] Hitler's ideas on propaganda were developed and his wish to reach an accommodation, in order to free Germany's hand in Eastern Europe, was stressed. The abridgment was silent on Germany's hostility to France, and this was so, Chamberlain speculated, because the German publisher did not wish to alienate English and American readers. The shortened version also left ample room for Hitler's anti-semitism.

A few days later, the former American Ambassador to Germany, James W. Gerard, analysed *My Battle* in historical perspective.[11] He argued that one could only understand the rise of Nazism in terms of the evolution of Germany since the Thirty Years War. Hitler embodied the German resentment over the Treaty of Versailles, her fear of another inflation, her wish to unite all Germans, and her reverence for militarism and hatred of communism. 'Even in the abridged translation there are pages and pages of attacks upon the Jews, but many more pages of such attacks were omitted and something of the spirit of the original was lost: much of the bitter prejudice and libel of the Jews.'

As in Great Britain, the book was widely reviewed by the leading American newspapers and magazines.[12] Among these were: *Saturday Review of Literature*; *New York Times*; *New York Herald Tribune*; *New York World-Telegram*; *American Mercury*; *Baltimore Sun*; *Dallas Times-Herald*; *North American Review*; *Chicago Daily News*; *St Louis Globe-Democrat*; *Louisville Courier-Journal*; *Los Angeles Times*; *Milwaukee Journal*; *Christian Science Monitor*; *Cleveland Plain Dealer*;

Kansas City Star; Springfield Sunday Union and Republican.
Even the general summaries sometimes echoed earlier protests,
witness the following from the *Kansas City Star*.[13] 'In spite of
letters of protest, accusation and threats of boycott and
bombing, Houghton Mifflin Company this week brought out
a translation of Adolf Hitler's warlike autobiography.'

Sales of *Mein Kampf* never lived up to Houghton Mifflin's
expectations.[14] Initially, 7,603 copies were printed in October
1933, selling at a retail price of $3.00. About 290 compliment-
ary copies were given away, and by the end of March 1934,
5,178 additional copies had been sold. Purchases then
dropped off considerably, according to the following figures.

Six months ending:	*Additional copies sold:*
30 Sept. 1934	457
31 March 1935	242
30 Sept. 1935	362
31 March 1936	359
30 Sept. 1936	575

The marginally increased sales from April to September 1936
may have reflected the growing concern for German rearmament stemming from their military occupation of the Rhineland in the previous March.

At the end of 1936 or beginning of 1937, the remaining 140
copies of the first edition were disposed of, thereby making it
possible to balance the account with Hitler's publisher, Eher
Verlag. The original contract had called for an author's
royalty of 15%, or 45 cents on each book sold. On the basis
of 7,313 copies, this amounted to gross royalties of $3,206.42
or the equivalent of RM8,487.22. As literary agent, the firm
of Curtis Brown was entitled to a commission of 20% on
gross royalties, and after that was deducted, the United
States Internal Revenue Service levied an additional 15%
corporation tax.[15] This left Eher Verlag with a net royalty on
the first American edition of $2,180.37 or RM5,668.96.

In spite of this edition's somewhat slow reception, Houghton Mifflin decided to hazard a second edition, which made its appearance in January 1937, reduced slightly in price to $2.50 and enhanced by a newly designed dust jacket. Instead of highlighting the Führer in stiff-armed salute against a black and white background, the refurbished jacket featured panels of red, black, and yellow, with contrasting letters and swastikas and a provocative quotation on its back by the columnist and author, Dorothy Thompson.

Within a month the dust jacket formed the basis of a diplomatic protest by the German government. The colour scheme was perceived as a calculated insult to the Nazi regime. Did not Houghton Mifflin realize that black, red, and gold were the colours of the detested Weimar Republic as well as those of the short-lived democratic experiment of the Frankfurt Parliament in 1848–9? Under the Second Empire of William I and Bismarck, these colours were repudiated and replaced by black, white, and red. Then, when Hitler overthrew the Republic in 1933, he insisted on identifying his Third Reich with the Second, accordingly restoring the imperial black, white, and red, superimposed with the Nazi swastika.

The quotation by Dorothy Thompson on the back of the dust jacket gave equal offence. The German Consul in Boston complained to the Ambassador in Washington.[16] 'The attempt of our former friend and now bitter enemy, Dorothy Thompson, to contribute a Preface to the volume has at least been rejected by Houghton Mifflin & Co., but a short excerpt from the draft introduction has been printed on the back of the book jacket in the interests of promoting sales.' The allusion to 'our former friend' went back to 1932 when Hitler favoured the American journalist with a private interview. She immediately rushed into print with a book entitled *I Saw Hitler* that greatly annoyed the Führer. He took his revenge in August 1934 by expelling her from the country. For the remainder of the decade she proclaimed her implacable opposition to the regime, using her thrice-weekly column in the *New York Herald Tribune*, 'Let the Record Speak', to vilify Hitler and his policies.

It is scarcely surprising that the German government took exception to Miss Thompson's statement, since it had been given to understand that Houghton Mifflin would represent the interests of the German author, Adolf Hitler. On the dust jacket the offensive quotation read:

As a liberal and democrat I deprecate every idea in this book. But it is not the function of liberals and democrats to live in a world of illusions. The principles, ideas, and policies laid down in this book have been followed with remarkable consistency by its author, who today controls the destinies of one of the greatest of the world powers.

The reading of this book is a duty for all who would understand the fantastic era in which we live, and particularly it is the duty of all who cherish freedom, democracy and the liberal spirit. Let us know what it is that challenges our civilization.

Houghton Mifflin hastened to assure the German government that no insult had been intended. During March 1937 several conferences took place between representatives from Houghton Mifflin and Arthur P. Teele, the lawyer representing the German Consulate in Boston. Writing on behalf of the firm, Ira Rich Kent explained to Teele:[17] 'So far as the colors are concerned, their selection was entirely accidental, and we are very glad to substitute white for the gold.' He then went on to explain why the publisher had incorporated the statement from Dorothy Thompson:

When we originally prepared the jacket it was with the hope and desire that we might have for this advertising purpose a thoroughly favorable criticism to contrast with an unfavorable one, our purpose, as publishers, being, naturally, to promote the sale and distribution of the book as widely as possible. We tried to find this material, but were unable to obtain any from an authoritative source of advertising value. Consequently the jacket was put out with the Thompson statement alone as that in itself advocated the purchase of the book.

The sales of the book in the original printing had not been up to our expectations, and we believed that a new promotion effort, of which this jacket is an important part, was desirable in order to secure for the book the distribution that its importance un-questionably deserves.

In the course of negotiations, Teele suggested not only that Houghton Mifflin supplement the Thompson quotation with one which was more positive, but that a revised dust jacket be submitted to the German publishing firm of Eher Verlag for its approval. At this point Houghton Mifflin demurred, pointing out that they had never dealt directly with Eher Verlag but always through the literary agency of Curtis Brown, and also that any permission to quote from another source would have to be secured through this intermediary. The Germans suggested that Houghton Mifflin use a statement in the *New York Herald Tribune* attributed to Lloyd George following his visit to Germany in September 1936.[18] However, this quotation said nothing specific about *Mein Kampf,* and permission to use it was complicated and time-consuming. The 'case', so to speak, rested at this juncture, with Houghton Mifflin willing to be accommodating but refusing to eliminate the Dorothy Thompson passage. The German archives as well as those of the Boston firm are in-complete, and so there is no conclusive evidence as to whether changes were actually incorporated into future printings of this edition. The Company does have in its possession a copy of the original January 1936 dust jacket, containing the offending gold or yellow colouring, but no example of a modified jacket has come to light.

Houghton Mifflin's decision to reissue *Mein Kampf* proved wise as far as sales were concerned. For the six months ending

31 March 1937 1,170 copies were sold, and during the following half-year another 1,451 were disposed of. Then there was a slackening off, so that by the spring of 1938, a total of 3,497 of the so-called popular edition had been sold, yielding gross royalties of $1,311.38 at the rate of $37\frac{1}{2}$ cents per copy. Once Curtis Brown's commission and the corporation tax were deducted, net royalties amounted to $891.74 or RM2,318.52.

International events then began to play a part in sales. The Nazis took over Austria in March 1938, and six months later Europe was on the brink of war. A renewed interest in Hitler manifested itself in the print orders for the latter half of 1938. Houghton Mifflin furnished dealers with 1,500 copies in August, a further 2,500 and 5,000 in October and another 5,000 in December. The year ending 31 March 1939 confirmed actual sales as 10,345, yielding gross royalties of $3,879.38, or net of $2,637.98 (RM6,858.74). Commenting on the increased sales of *Mein Kampf* in America during and after the Sudetenland crisis, one German newspaper observed:[19] 'Whenever the Führer is in the limelight of politics, the demand for the book increases.'

More than anything else, the Munich crisis in September 1938 aroused American suspicions concerning Hitler's reckless ambition. Perhaps the key to future Nazi policy lay buried in the pages of *Mein Kampf*. Several American publishers began to explore the possibility of issuing an unexpurgated edition, with or without the permission of Hitler's publisher in Germany. One of these firms was Reynal & Hitchcock, a relative newcomer to the New York publishing scene. In the winter of 1932–3 Eugène Reynal, who had his own reprint house of Blue Ribbon Books, and Curtice Hitchcock, formerly with the Century Book Company, had combined forces. Each had considerable experience in the trade, and for the rest of the 1930s they built up a promising list: a mixture of fiction, current affairs, travel, and history.

Reynal & Hitchcock described the stages by which they undertook to publish *Mein Kampf*:[20]

We felt, as early as September 1938, that it was imperative that an unabridged edition of this work be presented to the American public. We found that a translation of the unabridged work was being prepared by certain noted German scholars under the supervision of Dr. Alvin Johnson, Director of the New School for Social Research of New York. We found that leading historians and publicists were interested in having an edition of this work in English published in this country. We therefore suggested such publication to a distinguished group of sponsors . . . Upon securing their approval of the publication, we approached Houghton Mifflin Company and asked for the privilege of publishing an unabridged edition of the work. As the American copyrights were owned by Houghton Mifflin Company, the work, in our opinion, would not lawfully be published without their permission, and so we entered into a contract of lease with that company, whereby we acquired the right to publish an unabridged edition of the work on a royalty basis.

One of the aforementioned distinguished publicists was Raoul de Roussy de Sales, a French correspondent for *Paris Soir* who was a member of the French Consulate in New York and the President of the Association of Foreign Press Correspondents in the United States. Mrs Curtice Hitchcock recalls that: 'Raoul de Roussy de Sales, in his *Making of Yesterday*, several times mentions a dinner club to which my husband also belonged', and speculates that the idea of an unexpurgated *Mein Kampf* may well have germinated among these club members.[21] Another sponsor of the project, Graham Hutton, who was then foreign editor of *The Economist* in London, elaborated on this possibility. 'The edition took shape, I believe, from a suggestion by Dorothy Thompson and John Gunther, probably prompted by Raoul de Roussy de Sales . . . who moved around with all of us before the war, strongly anti-appeasement, friendly with all of the *Chicago Daily News* foreign correspondents.'[22]

An Editorial Committee of ten finally took shape, headed by Alvin Johnson, and including the well-known historians, Sidney B. Fay of Harvard University, Carleton J. H. Hayes of Columbia University, and William L. Langer of Harvard. Leading journalists were represented: John Chamberlain, editor of *Fortune* and literary critic for *Harper's Magazine*; John Gunther, freelance author and former foreign correspondent for the *Chicago Daily News*; Graham Hutton; Walter Millis, editorial and staff writer for the *New York Herald Tribune*; Raoul de Roussy de Sales; and George N. Shuster, former editor of *Commonweal* and soon to be President of Hunter College. Alvin Johnson was an academic economist by training, an associate editor of *New Republic* from 1917–22, and director of the New School for Social Research until 1945. He was an associate editor of the *Encyclopedia of the Social Sciences* from 1928 to 1934. Towards the end of the 1930s he made his reputation among liberals by facilitating the escape and relocation of European scholars fleeing from Nazi Germany.

This editorial board assumed more than a merely nominal role in the preparation of the text. In the Introduction it was noted:[23] 'We have, therefore, felt it our duty to accompany the text with factual information which constitutes an extensive critique of the original. No American would like to assume responsibility for giving the public a text which, if not tested in the light of diligent inquiry, might convey the impression that Hitler was writing history rather than propaganda.' To do this, they undertook two major editorial tasks: to mark the unabridged text so that readers could readily identify the portions which had been omitted from the Dugdale translation of 1933, and to furnish an elaborate commentary on the text, augmenting Hitler's 320,000 words with a further 80,000. The previous writings done by the members of the Committee testified to the expertise of its editors. In 1932 Shuster published *The Germans, an Inquiry and an Estimate*, followed in 1934 by *Strong Man Rules: An Interpretation of Germany Today*, and a year later by *Like a Mighty Army: Hitler Versus Established Religion*. In 1936 Gunther came out with his soon-to-be-famous *Inside Europe* and Hutton issued *Is It Peace?*, while in the following year Millis' *Viewed Without Alarm: Europe Today* made its appearance.

Some members were more nominal than active. Hutton writes: 'I do not recall Carleton Hayes or W. L. Langer having much to do with the project, as indeed I myself didn't and couldn't . . .'[24] Langer does not even remember having been on the Committee at all![25] Hutton felt that the bulk of the work fell to George Shuster, Alvin Johnson, and the translator, Helmut Ripperger: 'This inner ring would check with Dorothy and others of us who were available on specific points as they came up. But I don't think many came up. The work was heavy, continuous, skilled and concentrated on this inner ring.'

Shuster readily admits his heavy involvement in the project. 'Alvin Johnson . . . was an ardent opponent of Adolf Hitler. Since I was likewise one, we had come to know each other well even before my return from Europe in 1938.'[26] He and his wife were in Austria at the time of the Nazi takeover, and because he had spent a great deal of time in Germany over the years, he was chosen by Johnson to prepare the notes to the forthcoming edition:

The other members of the Committee did not write any of the notes. They met three times I believe and the discussion was both interesting and valuable. Not every member was very vocal, and only a few wrote letters which I was free to use or not.

About the middle of December 1938, Shuster began to feel a sense of pressure surrounding the completion of the edition:

85

I had a six weeks deadline. I remember that I spread notes on my German experiences on our living room floor and used them as I went along. I didn't have much trouble with my committee, excepting one American member. He thought I was too concerned with Catholics, and this was to some extent true, because my grant was for a study of the Center Party.

At the same time, the text of the translation was being revised:

The translation was made by some very able refugee scholars, members of the Faculty of the New School. But the language was quite Germanic in tone, and so Reynal & Hitchcock employed a professional translator to revise the text. But the time allotted was very brief; and so the poor man almost suffered a nervous breakdown trying to get his job done in time.

The 'poor man' in question was Helmut Ripperger, who had had considerable experience abroad. Following graduation from Fordham College, he had entered the Army Medical Corps during the First World War and remained abroad. He did public relations work for Thomas Masaryk of Czechoslovakia, edited the *Berlin Evening News*, and was, from 1923 to 1927, an American Vice-Consul in Bremen. During the 1930s he was employed in New York by Oxford University Press as a specialist in music, and in 1938 he also became a consultant to the Japanese Reference Library.

The sense of pressure felt by Ripperger, Shuster, and ultimately Reynal & Hitchcock, was not merely from a lack of sufficient time to handle their respective tasks adequately, or their wish to hurry a potential best-seller into the market. It was rather dictated by the fact that another American firm, Stackpole Sons Inc., suddenly challenged Houghton Mifflin's right to lease the copyright to Reynal & Hitchcock. More than this, Stackpole denied the validity of Houghton Mifflin's copyright in America on the grounds that Hitler had been a man without a country, a stateless individual, when he first published *Mein Kampf* in Germany, and only a German citizen could transfer his copyright to an American firm. Stackpole Sons had therefore announced their decision to publish the full text of *Mein Kampf* on 8 December 1938. Reynal & Hitchcock were taken completely by surprise, and felt their position very precarious because they had not yet negotiated a formal lease agreement with Houghton Mifflin.

On 12 December a conference was convened at the office of Reynal & Hitchcock, and Stackpole Sons' executive editor, William Soskin, defended his company's decision. The scene was later described by Edward J. Stackpole, a Brigadier General in the Pennsylvania National Guard and head of his family's firm:[27]

At this conference Mr. Soskin stated that we contemplated proceedings to nullify the alleged copyright of 'Mein Kampf' and put it into the public domain. Messrs. Reynal and Hitchcock, who attended this conference, told Mr. Soskin that if we could put the work into the public domain, they would not be interested in publishing an unexpurgated edition in competition with ours, and we would be free to go ahead. Acting on that, Mr. Soskin reported to me and I ordered the book immediately placed in the publishing processes. Translators were engaged and arrangements were made to set the book in type as the translation progressed. Paper was ordered for printing, and the facilities of our large plant were placed at the disposition of this book so that it might be available to the American public during the European crisis created by Hitler.

Reynal & Hitchcock's version was somewhat different.[28] They reminded Soskin that they had been engaged on the project for several months, that they had a translation in hand, that the assistance of an impressive Editorial Committee had been enlisted, and that they soon hoped to complete negotiations with Houghton Mifflin.

Soskin, however, left the conference convinced that Reynal & Hitchcock had backed away from the undertaking and that

Stackpole was free to go ahead. General Stackpole amplified this point:[29]

On the 27th day of December 1938, Mr. Hitchcock came to our office in New York and saw our Mr. Soskin. He then, for the first time, told Mr. Soskin that despite his previous statement to the contrary, he had now decided to go ahead with an unexpurgated edition of 'Mein Kampf' and that he had been in touch with Houghton Mifflin Company, who had assured him that their rights were exclusive. Mr. Soskin, at that time, told him that this was contrary to his expressed intention, and that he felt that he had been led to publish according to his understanding with Messrs. Reynal & Hitchcock.

We had in the meantime, investigated the status of Adolf Hitler and copyright registration of 'Mein Kampf', and were convinced that no exclusive rights existed in the book, and thereupon determined to go ahead.

As it turned out, Reynal & Hitchcock did not finally sign their lease agreement with Houghton Mifflin until 18 February 1939, a scant ten days before publication.[30] Houghton Mifflin as Lessor, 'warrants that it owns the United States volume rights in English to the complete work by Adolf Hitler', and 'in the event of any infringement, or threatened infringement, of said copyrights, the Lessor shall institute and prosecute such immediate proceedings in law or in equity as may be necessary . . .'. Houghton Mifflin agreed to pay 'all the expense of such proceedings wherein an injunction is sought, and the Lessor and the Lessee shall share equally in all of the expense of such proceedings brought solely for the recovery of damages'. Reynal & Hitchcock had the right to lease the work for three years, and were obliged to pay Houghton Mifflin a royalty of fifteen per cent on a list price of $3.00 per copy. Houghton Mifflin could continue issuing the abridged version, *My Battle*, but after one year Reynal & Hitchcock were given the option of producing a 'cheap edition' of the full text at a reduced price. Houghton Mifflin were given the exclusive right to print and bind the new work at their Riverside Press in Cambridge, Massachusetts.

One clause in the agreement almost led to difficulties:

The Lessee [Reynal & Hitchcock] agrees to provide a competent and scholarly English translation of the said work, complete with notes and such supplemental scholarly material as may be deemed advisable to include in the edition. It is agreed that nothing in said edition, whether notes, introduction, or general presentation, shall be deliberately hostile to the author, and that the spirit of the presentation shall be that of a highly important contemporary historical document. The Lessor shall have the right to examine and approve the entire work before it is published.

George Shuster explained the circumstances:[31]

We had trouble only with Houghton Mifflin Company, the representative of which was a true New Englander. I had known and liked him a great deal. But in Yankee fashion he insisted that Hitler was the Company's client and that nothing derogatory could therefore be said about him. For a moment it looked as if we were in great trouble. But Alvin Johnson, who was a past master of dealing with such matters and I (I had known the man for some time because of the Council of Foreign Relations) agreed to striking out a passage dealing with Hitler's relations with his niece, Geli Raubal.

Thus, in early 1939, both Reynal & Hitchcock and Stackpole Sons were frantically preparing their respective editions of *Mein Kampf* for the press, threatening each other with legal remedies and countermeasures, and trying to prepare the public for the anomaly of one authorized and one unauthorized version. At the same time Houghton Mifflin began to prepare for the inevitable legal confrontation by enlisting the support of Hitler's German publisher, Eher Verlag. Repeated requests for cooperation were made, but were only answered by impenetrable bureaucratic silence. As we have seen, Eher Verlag was at a loss as to what course to take and had called upon the Foreign Ministry, as well as upon the Party Chancellery, for guidance. It would be some months until a decision was made, and in the meantime Houghton Mifflin wondered whether, in addition to fighting Stackpole in the courts, they would also have to carry on a rearguard action against an irate German government intent upon quashing both unexpurgated editions in America.[32]

V

The Stackpole challenge

On 28 January 1939 Houghton Mifflin sought a permanent injunction against the Stackpole edition, claiming, among other things, that because the Stackpole firm 'was a corporation of small financial resources, only recently organized . . . the plaintiffs feared that it would be unable to respond in damages to any substantial degree'.[1] Moreover, it was argued that if the injunction were delayed, and Stackpole Sons sold very many copies, their potential liability might exceed their assets. To substantiate this claim they submitted a confidential report compiled by Dun and Bradstreet to the Federal Court for the Southern District of New York. During the ensuing legal proceedings, much came to light concerning the nature and extent of Stackpole's business.

According to the testimony, Stackpole Sons Inc. was 'a Pennsylvania corporation chartered May 2, 1938, with an authorized capital of $5,000, divided into 50 shares of common stock, $100 par value. The purpose of the organization was stated as a general printing and publishing business'.[2] Three men – E. J. Stackpole, A. H. Stackpole, and B. A. Brown – started the firm, but all of the shares were owned by the Telegraph Press of Harrisburg, Pennsylvania, whose President was Gen. Edward J. Stackpole, and whose Treasurer was B. A. Brown. The Telegraph Press was responsible for all of the printing and binding of Stackpole publications, although the firm maintained a sales office in New York at 250 Park Avenue.

91

The 1938 incorporation date is somewhat misleading, in that Gen. Stackpole actually launched his trade book venture in 1936 with the hiring of William Soskin as executive editor. Soskin had had considerable editorial experience. In 1927–8 he was the news editor for the *New York Evening Post*, and became its literary editor and critic from 1928 to 1933. From 1934 until he joined Stackpole, he was literary critic for the *New York American*, and continued as a contributing critic to the *New York Herald Tribune*. His book reviews and articles impressed Gen. Stackpole, paving the way for his appointment as head of the New York office.

Not brought out in the court hearing, but worthy of note, was the fact that shortly before its incorporation, Stackpole's New York office, for reasons of economy, not only let go one of its junior editors, but also its sales manager, George Stewart. Stewart's replacement was Virginia Mussey, who later married Soskin. She has reported: 'The New York office of Stackpole Sons was not doing well, but then, I think it was not doing badly either.'[3] Five thousand dollars capitalization was not very impressive, even by Depression standards, and taking into account limited liability, the company was indeed vulnerable to the imputation that it could not sustain a large damages suit.

Mrs Soskin has gone on to explain:

The formula then was that it took about five to seven years to build up a backlist active and productive enough to carry the overhead and produce some working capital, but to get through those first years took capital. Capital was what General Stackpole was reluctant to risk. There was always a tug-of-war between General Stackpole and my husband on that subject. The more basic fact is that a man named Brown who was, I believe, treasurer of the Telegraph Press and other Stackpole enterprises, had a low opinion of General Stackpole's venture into risky trade book publishing. He approved of the comfortable security and profit of the Military Publishing Company housed in the Telegraph Press building, and a magazine published by the Telegraph Press on trotting horses. This was dear to his heart as Mr. Brown was a trotting horse enthusiast and I believe owned and raised trotting horses himself.

In any case, Stackpole Sons, the trade book house, was building well. It had an excellent reputation in the trade with a good and growing list of saleable books. Bill [Soskin] had, after all, superb connections in the newspaper world, and from his years as a book reviewer, many in the literary world.

There was little doubt in George Stewart's mind that there were sufficient assets behind the combined Stackpole enterprises: 'Gen. Stackpole was very wealthy and the Telegraph Press very successful.'[4] For his part, Gen. Stackpole scoffed at the insinuation that his financial situation was the least bit shaky:[5]

My family have been active in publishing affairs in Pennsylvania for generations past. We are thoroughly solvent and do not need any small profits which can be made through the publication of any one book. On the contrary, we regard this as a publication venture of high social importance . . . The Telegraph Press does a general printing, photo-engraving, and publishing business, including among other things the official Legislative printing for the State of Pennsylvania.

The *Harrisburg Telegraph*, a daily newspaper dating back to 1831, was also owned by Gen. Stackpole, and furthermore, the Telegraph Press published a large number of school books for the State.

Stackpole Sons Inc. was thus a speculative offshoot of the Telegraph Press, with all of its expenses covered by the parent company, and there was no doubt that the Press could afford an all-out legal struggle even with a large and well-established firm like Houghton Mifflin. Among the growing list of Stackpole's publications, *How to Lose Friends and Alienate People* by Irving Tressler was the most successful. Others were Vincent McHugh's novel, *Caleb Catlum's America* and

Hitler's *Mein Kampf* in Britain and America

Orrick Johns' *Time of Our Lives, the Story of My Father and Myself*. Anthologies like Barrows Mussey's *We Were New England*, and biographies such as Edgar Johnson's *One Mighty Torrent: The Drama of Biography*, took their place beside volumes about history and current affairs. As one advertisement put it: 'Stackpole books are always news in that they are off the beaten track of publishing.'[6]

According to Virginia Soskin, the decision to publish *Mein Kampf* originated with her husband:[7]

If my memory is correct, Bill Soskin came to the idea of publishing an unabridged edition in English of *Mein Kampf* after a lunch with Dorothy Thompson, whose *The Intelligent Woman's Guide to Politics* Stackpole had published. I cannot give you the date of this luncheon, but I should guess it was perhaps six months or so earlier than the publication date. Philip Wittenberg, our lawyer in the case, had to be consulted, and a great many other details worked out.

Soskin viewed the publication of *Mein Kampf* as an opportunity to improve the prospects of Stackpole's New York office:[8]

Mein Kampf was a significant title on the Stackpole list as indeed it would have been on the list of any publisher in this country at that time. Of course it would (and did) give Stackpole's still further distinction – again, as it would any publisher: a best-seller on any publisher's list was a great boost to the house and always increased sales of other titles on the same list.

Wittenberg confirmed that Soskin initiated and carried forward the project: 'It was he who became interested in the publication of *Mein Kampf*. Most of the work I did was done by and through him. You are correct in assuming that the decision was made following the Munich crisis.'[9]

Once the decision to go ahead with *Mein Kampf* was made in early December 1938, the very practical problem of a translation bulked large. Reynal & Hitchcock already had a rough translation, whereas Stackpole had to start from scratch. The most obvious person for Soskin to approach was Barrows Mussey, the junior editor whom he had let go the previous February, and who had facility in twelve foreign languages. Mussey described the curious relationship he had with the firm following his dismissal:[10]

For a time Soskin and I remained on tolerable terms; I translated a novel by Heinrich Hauser for him while launching myself as a professional translator of various languages . . . The scuffling began when Curtice Hitchcock and Eugène Reynal . . . cooked up a deal with Houghton Mifflin (I think Henry Laughlin was the active figure) for Reynal & Hitchcock to take a license for a new edition in which they would not be bound by the Houghton Mifflin restriction. At the same time someone . . . put Soskin on to the idea of claiming that Hitler's copyright was void. He thereupon asked me if I would do the translation at a speed to beat out Reynal & Hitchcock.

My position was amusing in that I had known and liked Reynal & Hitchcock for years, and further their translation was . . . by Helmut Ripperger, also an old friend – whom I had previously hired to put in order a Spanish Civil War novel that Whittaker Chambers had abandoned translating part way through, and that I had to finish – and previously an apartment mate of George Stewart and Karl Küp of the New York Public Library.

Furthermore, it was awkward because Mussey had recently divorced Virginia, the current Stackpole sales manager. By late 1938, however, Mussey had remarried, moved out of New York City, and needed the money. He remembers being paid at the then going rate of $5 per thousand words, or a total of about $1,500. He ensconced himself in the top floor of a house 'the ground floor of which was a nursery school operated by my second wife and her sister. I rented and then bought a used Ediphone wax-cylinder dictating machine. I found that while I couldn't work much faster than on a type-writer, I could keep at it longer.' He preferred working in the middle of the night: 'an idiosyncrasy left over from my childhood dislike of being sent to bed. I seem to remember setting myself a stint of twenty pages a day.' He hired a 'very pretty and very plump young public stenographer' to transcribe the Ediphone cylinders. One of the hazards of her transcribing such material came out in her remark: 'Gosh, I never realized before why Hitler had to do that to the Jews.' He would spend the mornings revising the previous day's work and then resume his wearisome labour in the evenings. Soon people began to talk. 'Thus neighbours late at night could hear a voice barking out indignant abuse of the Jewish people, and the word got around . . . that Mussey's wife had married a guy who was a little touched, and was not let out of the attic.'[11]

As to the problems of translating *Mein Kampf*, he mused:[12]

Someone (I rather think Hilaire Belloc) said the supreme test of a translator was truly rendering a bad book; I agree, and would add my own observation, 'there's nothing you get so sick of as a good job well done'.

Mein Kampf is a bad, a semi-literate book, but a book all the same, with something to say. The difficulty of course was in how Hitler said it: like any politician he had a stock of blank-check words, which wanted matching to analogous English vapidities. As a time-saving device I made a card index with as many equivalents as possible for each German word.

Even using these shortcuts, the task seemed interminable. Other ways to speed things up were tried:

Well, with time and Reynal & Hitchcock pressing, Soskin got a woman named something like Katz to translate the last two-fifths or so of the book, alleging that I could fix it up faster than do it new.

I learned then a dismaying though valuable fact that I had previously suspected but never proved: to revise an unusually competent translation takes as long as doing it from scratch, since you have to work through the same processes of grasping, transposing and formulation.

Mussey finally dropped the chore, and to this day has 'never read the rest of *Mein Kampf*. Possibly Soskin and Virginia worked it over in the office.' Mrs Soskin, once a translator of children's books, later confirmed that she had been pressed into service:[13]

We were in a dead-heat race with Reynal & Hitchcock to get our respective editions to the booksellers first and if we could, before the lower court handed down its decision. I therefore completed the last pages of the translation in an unconscionably short time – a week perhaps. I was under tremendous pressure but aside from being weary, I can remember having difficulty only with some of Hitler's portmanteau words and I remember calling a German friend who knew English very well to ask him the meaning for one of them – the word for *poster* I think.

When the book was finally ready for publication, Mussey staunchly refused to have his name mentioned either in the volume itself or in publicity releases, explaining:[14]

My uneasy truce with Soskin, meanwhile, had turned to an abiding hatred, which was the main reason I wouldn't put my name on the book. Another reason was that I had pre-Hitler friends in Germany and others in New York who might have been annoyed or affected. One, Ernest Eisele, for many decades the head of the Westermann book store in New York, had wanted me to sign a translation of some official German publication, which I also declined for the countervailing reason that it would have sat badly with my numerous Jewish associates.

Soskin was justifiably disappointed by this last-minute refusal, but did his best to turn the anonymity into an advantage. Some advertisements noted that: 'The Stackpole translation has been done by a scholar and well-known translator of many German books, who prefers to remain anonymous because of personal connections in present day Germany.'[15]

Following publication of the two competing editions on 28 February 1939, Reynal & Hitchcock and Stackpole lost no opportunity to discredit the other's translation. Helmut Ripperger, the translator of the Reynal & Hitchcock version, wrote a letter to *Publishers' Weekly* contending that Stackpole's translation was based not on the first German edition, as the publisher claimed, but on one of the later and revised German editions.[16] Soskin admitted having used a later edition, but insisted that discrepancies between it and the original had been accounted for. Mrs Soskin acknowledges this:[17]

I can remember that I spent many hours in the Rare Book Room of the New York Public Library restoring to the text of the edition we were using for the translation the changes and deletions made from the original, first German edition. The NYPL had the only copy of the first edition anywhere in New York City.

She added, as a personal reflection: 'When I read the first chapters of *Mein Kampf* in the New York Public Library one morning before I went out to lunch, I remember running down the long flight of steps to Fifth Avenue and reaching the curb just in time to vomit. I have since considered that the definitive review of the book.' Mussey recalls one occasion when he wished to check personally on a particular passage in the original. 'I went to the NYPL and asked to see the first edition, but found it was not available. Curtice Hitchcock later smirked at this . . .'[18] Mussey suspects that Ripperger's friend, Karl Küp, had seen to it that the first German edition was temporarily inaccessible. Ripperger, on the other hand, had access to *three* copies of the first German edition, thanks to the refugee translators at the New School for Social Research.

In its publicity, Stackpole made much of Houghton Mifflin's failure to issue the full text of *Mein Kampf*. Soskin stressed this point in a letter to the editor of *Publishers' Weekly*:[19]

It is an important fact in this situation that the publishers of a radically abridged edition, which appeared in 1933, did not announce publication, nor intent to publish the complete text, despite overwhelming demands for it and despite many expressions from scholars, historians and scientists, until some three weeks after Stackpole Sons' public announcement that they would go ahead with publication.

Even after Stackpole's announcement Houghton Mifflin decided not to issue the complete text itself, but rather to lease the right to Reynal & Hitchcock. Many informed observers at the time presumed that this meant that Houghton Mifflin's contract with Eher Verlag applied solely to an abridgment and precluded publishing the full text. Mussey echoes this conviction: 'I do remember that Houghton Mifflin, urged to do a complete *Mein Kampf* as well as the previously authorized shortened version, said their contract with Hitler prevented it.'[20] As a result of the apparent consensus on this point, Soskin and his attorney, Philip Wittenberg, were sceptical regarding Houghton Mifflin's repeated assertion that their contract covered any American edition. As we have seen in Chapter III, Houghton Mifflin's 1933 contract did differ indeed from Hurst & Blackett's.

Notwithstanding the disputed contractual nuances, Wittenberg uncovered an even more damaging piece of evidence threatening Houghton Mifflin while on a trip to Washington, D.C.:[21]

When we investigated and found that Hitler had taken his copyright as a stateless person, we were sure of our grounds. In fact, the Register of Copyrights, who was going over the cards with me in Washington, said when we came to the card, 'Well, there's your case.'

On the first application to secure copyright for Volume I of *Mein Kampf* dated 1925, Hitler was described as a 'stateless German' (*staatenlöser Deutscher*). In 1927, the application for Volume II indicated that he was an Austrian citizen. Soskin and Wittenberg were sure that they could prove that Hitler had given up his Austrian citizenship by 1925, while not acquiring German citizenship until 1932. They knew that section 8 of the Copyright Act of 1909 extended protection only to an 'author or proprietor who is a citizen or subject of a foreign state or nation' that granted to 'a citizen of the United States the benefit of copyright on substantially the same basis as to its own citizens'. Since Hitler by the mid-1920s was a man without a country, Soskin and Wittenberg were convinced that it was immaterial whether the United States had reciprocal copyright treaties with either Germany or Austria because he could not, under the circumstances, secure a valid copyright in America in any case.

At first, the weight of this argument staggered Reynal & Hitchcock. The initial consultation with a copyright lawyer seemed to support Stackpole. Highly distraught, Curtice Hitchcock sought the advice of Chauncey H. Hand, a partner in the New York law firm of Hines, Rearick, Dorr and Hammond, and a 'close personal friend'. 'It was Blink Hand, approaching the matter with the clarity of one who had never handled a copyright case, who read the legislation and saw the fallacy of the argument.'[22] Hand's partner, Archie O. Dawson, was subsequently retained by Houghton Mifflin to argue the case before the Federal District Court.

Despite Reynal & Hitchcock's momentary anxiety, Houghton Mifflin presumably never had any doubt that their 1933 contract included an unabridged edition. Therefore, their arrangement with Reynal & Hitchcock had nothing to do with the adequacy of their contract. Throughout the controversy, Houghton Mifflin maintained that the reasons for their not issuing an unabridged edition were purely commercial. These were never spelled out, but one may conjecture that the disappointing sales figures for the abridgment made them reluctant to speculate too heavily on the full text. The 1937 popular edition sold a bit more briskly but there was concern that the market was becoming saturated. Besides, Reynal & Hitchcock had a translation already prepared and were willing to risk a lease agreement whereby they could exploit whatever market still existed and pay Houghton Mifflin a royalty. Furthermore, as we have seen, Houghton Mifflin did the printing and binding of the full text, while still retaining the privilege of selling its abridged version. As far as Houghton Mifflin were concerned, the only loss they suffered was the prestige attached to bringing out the un-expurgated edition; it was definitely not a question of Nazi censorship. Mrs Hitchcock commented in a letter: 'Henry Laughlin often expressed regret that Houghton Mifflin had not thought of it themselves.'[23]

By January 1939 Houghton Mifflin and Reynal & Hitchcock had both become enormously frustrated by Stackpole's un-willingness to seek prompt legal action. It was apparent that the delay was intentional. A Stackpole newsletter sent to customers became part of the evidence which Houghton Mifflin submitted to the court:[24]

Stackpole Sons, having invited and received service in a suit to prove its right to publish the unexpurgated *Mein Kampf* which Adolf Hitler has censored in this country for five years, now announce positive publication for February 28. The nature of the suit is such that there can be no decision or obstacle to publication until the fall of 1939.

Stackpole's obvious procrastination spurred Houghton Mifflin's lawyers to seek a 'preliminary' or temporary injunc-tion, pending a decision granting a permanent one.

It was far from evident what Stackpole was gaining by such heel-dragging. Both parties were incurring substantial legal fees and inviting costly damages. Mrs Soskin later put her finger on Stackpole's apparent motive:[25]

Clearly everybody wanted to recoup as much of his investment in this *Mein Kampf* project as possible. The legal fees added to

101

translation fees, the possibility that Stackpole might be enjoined from selling the book soon after publication, the big investment in composition, printing, paper, etc., and in extra man-hours owing to the speed with which the job had to be done, sales were vital if we were not to have a huge loss.

In an affidavit to the District Court, Gen. Stackpole indicated that on the eve of publication their total expenses amounted to $21,000 for an initial impression of 15,000 copies.[26] Here, then, we find one of the peculiarities common to both Stackpole and Houghton Mifflin: each had its own printing establishment – not the usual thing for most publishing houses – and each wanted to sell enough copies to at least cover their printing costs before having to pay damages.

Among the surviving papers of Reynal & Hitchcock, there is a particularly revealing inter-office memo which Eugène Reynal sent out to salesmen and others on 17 February:[27]

I want to summarize for you the situation on *Mein Kampf* to date – and it is very important that communications in writing be kept strictly in our own hands.

1. The Legal Situation . . . We had reason to believe that Stackpole would hasten this action in order to have the matter cleared before publication, but since that time they have sent out a note for general circulation to the effect that action could be delayed so as to enable them to proceed with the publication of their book . . . If everything should go through promptly and if Stackpole really wants a quick adjudication, the legal situation may be cleared up before the publication date. I want to warn you, however, and you will have to warn the trade, that injunctions, particularly temporary ones, are extremely tricky and that in spite of our best efforts and the strength of our basic case, both editions may appear on the market. Also, I want to impress upon you that even if the temporary injunction is denied, it signifies nothing in regard to the ultimate disposition of the suit. It will be a great convenience if we can obtain it but, if not, it is to be treated as a matter of no importance.

2. The Boycott Situation. We have every reason to believe that

before very long we will get some sort of official approval of our edition from the various boycott committees, which will mean that the department stores, primarily the Jewish ones, will be entirely free to go ahead with a store-wide promotion of our book. One store in New York has indicated that they will take 5,000 copies provided there is no trouble from the boycott committees, and orders of this nature even if not as large I am sure can be obtained throughout the country.

Both firms hoped to avoid boycotts by promising to donate a portion of their respective profits to refugee organizations. In anticipation of a large sale, and to facilitate rapid distribution, Reynal & Hitchcock ordered an initial printing of 25,000 copies, followed as soon as possible by another 25,000. Under Point 4 in the above memorandum, Reynal covered the 'sales argument'.

The one effective selling point that Stackpole has is 'no royalties to Germany'. I am enclosing with this letter a reprint of the statement we made in the *Publishers' Weekly* and you should all carry a copy of these to leave with any customers who are in doubt about our position.

Soskin, in the meantime, wrote to the Old Corner Bookstore, upon learning that it had cancelled its order:[28]

I thought you would be interested to know that a recent test mailing made by Brentano's in New York who described both editions of *Mein Kampf* to their charge accounts, pointing out that one paid no royalties to Germany while the other did, received an immediate, overwhelming response, with the ratio of four-to-one in favor of the Stackpole edition.

Reynal sought to counter this as follows:

The answer to this argument, as you know, is the very simple one that there is no other legal way in which the book can be published without paying royalties to Germany. The actual royalties to be received will be less than 6%, from which it should be possible to deduct the costs of litigation. Stackpole is publishing in next week's

Publishers' Weekly the dirtiest announcement in this whole messy business. They claim that the only purpose that our litigation can serve is to take money from the refugees in order to turn it over to Hitler. This, like most of Stackpole's statements, is just plain not true.

One of the exhibits placed before the District Court added weight to Stackpole's intention to allocate a portion of its profit from *Mein Kampf* to various refugee organizations.[29] Such funds were to be handled by a committee whose membership included: Dr Harold Lasswell, the political scientist; Dr Wesley C. Mitchell, an economist from Columbia University; George Gordon Battle, attorney; Dr Reinhold Niebuhr of the Union Theological Seminary; Dr Horace M. Kallen of the New School for Social Research; Ernest Meyer, a columnist for the *New York Post*; Max Eastman, distinguished author; Dr Vida D. Schudder, Professor Emerita of Wellesley College; Dr Louis Hacker, an historian from Columbia University; Dr Benson Y. Landis of the Federal Council of Churches; Dr Allen Heely, Headmaster of Lawrenceville School; Dr Milton C. Winternitz, Professor of Pathology and former Dean of the Yale Medical School; and Dr Edward Smith Parons, President Emeritus of Marietta College. Contemporaries would have readily recognized most of these names as well-known leaders in the fields of religion and scholarship. Although this committee had nothing to do with the actual preparation of the book, it was obviously intended as a counter-force to offset the lustre of Reynal & Hitchcock's Committee of experts. Accordingly, Eugène Reynal felt obliged to reiterate praise for his firm's Committee and its chairman, Alvin Johnson:

Johnson's name is extremely important and the New School should be sufficient guarantee to anyone that the book is not pro-Hitler. . . . Stackpole have announced that they will donate 5% of their proceeds to a refugee fund after learning of our proposal. They are paying no royalties whatever. This amounts to little more than one-sixth of what we are paying in royalties alone. On the other hand, we are turning over all profits to the refugees after deducting our legitimate expenses, including approximately 25 % for general overhead, which is a figure considerably below the normal publishing overhead percentage.

The day after this long memorandum was circulated in the offices of Reynal & Hitchcock, Curtice Hitchcock composed a similar communication to be sent to Houghton Mifflin. Regarding the proposed fund for refugees, he emphasized that none of the assets would be touched nor any royalty be paid to Hitler's publisher 'until all legal issues in the case are finally determined, such proceeds shall be put in escrow in a special bank account in our name, subject to use as hereafter provided in meeting the possible extraordinary legal expense and damages hereafter mentioned'.[30]

On 28 February, the day on which the competing editions appeared, Judge Alfred Coxe of the Federal District Court denied Houghton Mifflin's motion for a temporary injunction:[31]

I do not think that this case is sufficiently clear to warrant the issuance of a preliminary injunction. The Defendants Stackpole have raised questions of title and validity which are not free from doubt; the facts are in dispute; and the issues cannot properly be determined on affidavits.

The facts 'in dispute' were those having to do with Hitler's citizenship during the 1920s. Stackpole were assiduous about supplying the District Court with extracts from German newspapers, both in the original and in translation, supporting the contention that Hitler consciously renounced his Austrian citizenship prior to 1925 and was unable to secure German citizenship for the next seven years. Both sides summoned legal experts in order to learn whether an Austrian citizen like Adolf Hitler automatically forfeited his citizenship upon enlisting in the German army in 1914.

105

We now know that following his abortive *putsch* in Munich in November 1923 and a year spent in prison, Hitler was determined to rid himself of Austrian citizenship. On several occasions the Bavarian Ministry of the Interior sought to expel him, but to Hitler's relief the Austrian government refused to admit such an undesirable alien. They claimed that he had presumably forfeited all right to Austrian citizenship by having enlisted in the German army at the beginning of the First World War. Furthermore, he had never shown any inclination to recover that citizenship thereafter. Bavaria would simply have to put up with such a trouble-maker.[32] Nonetheless, two months after being released from prison in December 1924, the state forbade Hitler to make any more public speeches. Taking alarm that this time he might be expelled from the country, he adhered to this imposition of silence. In addition he formally renounced his allegiance to Austria on 7 April 1925. Four years later his Nazi crony, Frick, tried to secure German citizenship for Hitler, but this backstairs manoeuvre failed. Not until February 1932 did he receive an appointment from the state of Brunswick which carried with it German citizenship – just in time to run for the Presidency of the Weimar Republic.

Since the question of the rights of a stateless individual to copyright in America had never come before the American courts, it was not surprising that Judge Coxe hesitated to issue an injunction. However, Houghton Mifflin refused to be daunted, and appealed Coxe's decision to the next level of Federal jurisdiction, the Second Circuit Court of Appeals. Several months thereby elapsed during which both Stackpole and Reynal & Hitchcock continued to sell as many copies of *Mein Kampf* as fast and furiously as they could. Curtice Hitchcock reported to Ferris Greenslet, Houghton Mifflin's Vice-President, that early sales were encouraging:[33]

All the dope we can get around New York is that our edition is outselling the other handsomely. The Doubleday shops report a ratio of ten to one or thereabouts, and others seem, if not quite as good, at least gratifying. I think we shall have about 5,000 copies of the new 10,000 sold by the time the stock gets in, making a total to date of around 30,000. There isn't quite the lift in the book that we had hoped for, but next week ought to provide new evidence.

Toward the end of March, Reynal & Hitchcock negotiated a highly gratifying arrangement with the Book of the Month Club. The 300,000 members would be notified that a special edition of *Mein Kampf* would be made available for $3.00. The Club's Vice-President, Meredith Wood, explained the terms to Curtice Hitchcock:[34]

We agree to pay you a royalty of 35 cents per copy for all copies of your edition of 'Mein Kampf' sold by us, and we further guarantee that the total of such per-copy royalties shall amount to a sum not less than $10,000. We agree to sell the book on a non-profit basis (as far as we are concerned) charging manufacturing costs, our selling expenses and other expenses directly attributable to the distribution by us of this book . . . We are to pay the balance of the receipts from the sale of the book to the Editorial Committee listed in the book, to be held in trust as a fund for refugees, which is to be distributed under their direction. We further guarantee that our payments to this refugee fund shall amount to a total of not less than $20,000.

By early June the Club acknowledged that it had overestimated the popularity of *Mein Kampf*, and therefore, instead of offering it as a Book of the Month, it would be listed as a premium to members.[35]

Royalties, profits on sales, and charitable contributions were all held in abeyance,[36] awaiting a decision in the courts. By fending off the opposition, Stackpole had perhaps won the first round, but the fight was far from over.

VI

Houghton Mifflin v. *Stackpole* on appeal

During the month of April 1939 Houghton Mifflin and Stackpole filed their respective briefs with the Second Circuit Court of Appeals. Although Houghton Mifflin continued to insist that Hitler was an Austrian citizen rather than a stateless person during the 1920s, this point was tacitly conceded by the Boston firm: 'The plaintiff, while contending that Hitler had not lost his Austrian citizenship at the time the copyrights were issued, nevertheless maintains that even if he were stateless, as contended by defendants–respondents, the copyrights would be valid.'[1]

Both parties then focused on three main issues. First, was a stateless person entitled to the benefit of copyright under the laws of the United States? Second, could it be satisfactorily shown or assumed that Hitler had assigned his rights in *Mein Kampf* to Eher Verlag of Munich? Third, had Houghton Mifflin acquired the sole rights to the American market or did they merely have a license to publish the work? The American Copyright Act of 1909 was silent on the question of stateless individuals, nor were there any court cases which provided precedents. Nevertheless, Houghton Mifflin found a relevant opinion dealing with the status of authors from the Philippines rendered by the United States Attorney-General in 1904. In that case, since Filipinos were neither citizens of a foreign state nor of the United States, they were, in effect, 'stateless'. However, the Attorney-General felt that the works of such writers were entitled to the protection of

American copyright law. Stackpole countered that this situation was special because it involved authors living within territorial possessions of the United States, not, technically, stateless individuals:[2]

Adolf Hitler was not a citizen of any country with which the United States had copyright relations at the time that Franz Eher Nachfolger applied for and received copyright . . . Only those non-resident aliens are protected who are citizens or subjects of countries coming within the provisions of Section 8 of the copyright law.

As to the second point, Stackpole claimed that Houghton Mifflin's title was 'defective' and that its rights were 'derivative' and 'secondary':[3]

There is no proof of an assignment of American copyright from Adolf Hitler to Franz Eher Nachfolger, the plaintiff–appellant's assignor . . . It is incumbent upon the plaintiff–appellant, therefore, to show that its assignor, Franz Eher Nachfolger, obtained its rights from the author, Adolf Hitler.

This claim was put forth knowing full well that it was next to impossible for Houghton Mifflin to produce a document proving that Eher Verlag had acquired Hitler's copyright back in 1925–7.

The third issue, concerning Houghton Mifflin's contract with Eher Verlag, involved certain technicalities which Stackpole eagerly sought to exploit. The 1933 contract had been signed by a representative of Houghton Mifflin while travelling abroad, and thus it came under Section 43 of the 1909 copyright statute which declared: 'every assignment of copyright executed in a foreign country shall be acknowledged by the assignor before a consular officer or secretary of legation of the United States authorized by law to administer oaths or perform notarial acts'.[4] Unfortunately, Houghton Mifflin had neglected to have their contract so notarized, and to complicate matters still more, no officer of Eher Verlag had signed the Houghton Mifflin copy of the contract. Instead, only the name of the firm was affixed. In addition, Stackpole argued that Houghton Mifflin had acquired only the 'book' rights to *Mein Kampf*, not the full rights to the work, including drama, cinema, and radio. Such partial rights constituted a license to publish in America, but a mere licensee could not seek an injunction and damages in an American court. This privilege was reserved to the proprietor of the copyright, which in this case was either Hitler or perhaps Eher Verlag, but certainly not Houghton Mifflin. The Boston firm disagreed, pointing out that the language of the 1933 contract was explicit: Eher Verlag was the 'proprietor' with power to 'assign' book rights to Houghton Mifflin.

On 18 May 1939 the case was brought before three judges of the Second Circuit Court of Appeals: Charles E. Clark, Learned Hand, and Augustus N. Hand. Both Learned Hand and his cousin had been on the Court of Appeals for more than a decade, while Clark was a newcomer to the Bench, having been appointed earlier that same year. Eventually Clark wrote the Opinion in this case, and so it is perhaps appropriate to examine his background in some detail. A graduate from Yale University in 1911, he remained there for two more years and took his law degree. In 1919 he returned to the Yale Law School as an Assistant Professor, and within a few years was promoted to full Professor. Sometime along the way he switched from the Republican to the Democratic Party and became increasingly involved in state and national politics. In 1929 he was chosen to succeed Robert Maynard Hutchins as Dean of the Yale Law School. Clark became a staunch supporter of Franklin D. Roosevelt during the early years of the New Deal, even supporting the President's controversial plan to expand the membership of the Supreme Court.

Following the hearing of *Houghton Mifflin* v. *Stackpole* on appeal, the three justices prepared for their conference scheduled for 24 May, when a decision would be reached. To help prepare his 'pre-conference Memorandum', Judge Clark had the assistance of a young law clerk, Elizabeth R. Horan. She first addressed herself to the question of whether a stateless individual could secure a valid American copyright: 'I think, first, that Plaintiff [Houghton Mifflin] should prevail on its point 1, and that it would be desirable for this Court to say so even if it should uphold defendant on some other point.'[5] She admitted that 'stateless persons were not much of a problem' in the past, and as far as the rights of American authors abroad were concerned, 'stateless aliens were and are unimportant and impotent'. Next, she turned her attention to the issue of whether Hitler had duly transferred his rights in *Mein Kampf* to Eher Verlag, acknowledging that 'there is not much to go on' in support of Houghton Mifflin, 'but I think there is enough. Plaintiff's allegations "on information and belief" are all right, and Defendant's denial is not enough to upset the *prima facie* made out by the complaint *plus* exhibits and affidavits.' She acknowledged that it was odd that the copyright was not assigned 'before a consular officer as provided in section 43 of the copyright statute', and added that it 'is not much good' to provide an affidavit after the fact, as the President of Houghton Mifflin did.

As to the third issue of licensing Houghton Mifflin to publish, she wrote:

I think Plaintiff's other arguments showing that its assignor had the proper rights as proprietor are sensible. No one can suppose the book could be published in Germany or U.S. copyright obtained without the author's consent. I should think the Court might even take judicial notice of that. Nor do I think the defendant's argument that Plaintiff is just a licensee makes sense. Plaintiff is surely right in saying that a political treatise could only be published.

Finally, assuming that *Mein Kampf* had no potential as theatre or cinema material, Miss Horan concluded:

111

Hitler's *Mein Kampf* in Britain and America

I do not see any dispute of facts to support Judge Coxe's decision denying temporary injunction. It seems to me that all Plaintiff needed was a *prima facie* case and they have that. Defendant's affidavits are all concerned with showing Hitler's lack of citizenship. Maybe there is a dispute here, but if this fact is assumed to be as Defendant contends, there is no reason for denying the injunction on the ground of dispute of facts. The other questions of fact – the 'proprietor's' rights and execution of the assignment are not really disputed either. There is nothing but inference and bare denial to dispute the Plaintiff's allegations, and the evidence of the U.S. copyrights obtained by the German publisher and the assignment. In plain fact, it is impossible to imagine that the German publisher could act in any way contrary to the author's wishes . . . I confess that I think the equities are strongly with the Plaintiff. Defendant is trying to take advantage of the anti-Hitler feeling in the U.S. Suppose the author was a 'stateless' German Jew, and other facts were the same? Nowadays that might be the best case – except that Stackpole would not be foolish enough to try the same racket.

Judge Clark's pre-conference Memorandum incorporated many of his clerk's views. In light of the growing number of refugees who were victims of Hitler's tyranny, he reiterated: 'I think it would be a terrible thing to deny these homeless persons even literary property nowadays, and I shall not want to come to it unless forced to come and therefore I am glad to see myself forced the other way.'[6] Clark was troubled by the failure of Houghton Mifflin to have its contract notarized in 1933, but reasoned: 'I should suppose that under our ordinary law of assignments, the document at the very least conveys an equitable title good against strangers' like Stackpole. As to Eher Verlag's right to assign the copyright of *Mein Kampf* to Houghton Mifflin:

I think that Plaintiff had full rights as assignee anyway, and even as partial assignee should be recognized to sue. It would certainly be stupid to hold in the present condition of Germany that Hitler's publishers have no rights in his literary property while the government makes newly married couples, school children, and the like buy the book . . . There are no equities at all in favor of the Defendants' barefaced attempt to make money hastily, except possibly an appeal to patriotism. And wasn't it Samuel Johnson who characterized that adequately? Certainly it seems to me that a *prima facie* showing in behalf of the Plaintiff has been made, and it is not sufficient to say, as does Coxe, J., that there are matters of title in dispute. There is not enough dispute to say that the Defendants are entitled to sell with impunity now on the idea that the Plaintiff may collect later if it can.

I vote to reverse.

Learned Hand's pre-conference Memorandum came to grips with section 8 of the 1909 Copyright Act:[7]

The Section does not confine the privilege to citizens or subjects of a sovereign; it confers it upon 'authors' generally; the rest of it is in limitation of this general grant. It provides that when a man is a subject or a citizen of a foreign sovereign, he has the privilege 'only' in case he is domiciled within the United States, or in case the sovereign, to whom he owes his allegiance, grants reciprocal privileges to citizens of the United States. The fact that Congress was slow to extend copyright to authors other than citizens of the United States, does not mean that, when in 1891 it changed its mind, it meant to exclude those who have no allegiance whatever. There is no reason why it should have so intended, for their exclusion cannot coerce any other sovereign to grant copyright to citizens of the United States. True, there is no authority on this except the opinion of the Attorney-General, but that goes for something . . .

As to the copyright owner's title, it would be rather absurd for us to hold that there was no evidence of any assignment by Hitler to the Franz Eher Company. Hitler has been the dictator of Germany since 1933, shortly after the supposed assignment! The Franz Eher Company has issued millions and millions of copies of the book. We cannot with any sense refuse to recognize that a man in absolute power would not have allowed this unless the publisher had the right. This may not be sufficient evidence on final hearing, but we are dealing with a preliminary injunction, where there is no dispute, but merely a demand for formal proof.

I vote to reverse.

On the question of statelessness and the American copyright law, Augustus Hand agreed with his judicial colleagues:[8]

If I had to decide the question whether 'Adolf the Fair' could obtain a United States copyright I should say that such a lovely fellow as the 'Staatenlöser Deutscher' came within the broad, free-for-all clause of the copyright act, and not the concluding exception. The decision of the Copyright Office on such a matter ought to be given great weight since it interprets the scope of an act as to which it has expert knowledge. Moreover, as long ago as 1904, it had before it the opinion of the Attorney-General as to applications by the inhabitants of the Philippines – an opinion that at least seems to me sensible.

However, Augustus Hand strongly differed from his fellow judges when it came to the other main issues of the case:

I think we ought not to pass on the capacity of Adolf to father an American copyright when there is no better proof that a German concern which assigned its rights to the Plaintiff was the real proprietor. Whether it was depends on whether Adolf wrote the book and assigned his rights to the Plaintiff. There is nothing but an unverified assertion in the complaint [by Houghton Mifflin] that he did either. I think the Plaintiff ought to have more proof than an assertion that Hitler wrote the book (an assertion that he would deny any day in two seconds if he chose to) and that he assigned his right to the German publisher. The provision of 17 U.S. Code section 55 that the certificate of registration of a copyright is '*prima facie* evidence of the facts stated therein' does not help the Plaintiff, for the certificate does not state the so-called proprietor is the owner, but only designates him as the 'claimant' of the copyright.

I vote to affirm the order denying a preliminary injunction.

In the Court's Opinion, dated 9 June 1939, Judge Clark

reiterated much of what had been articulated a few weeks before, describing the 1933 contract between Houghton Mifflin and Eher Verlag as 'a General Department Royalty Contract, an extensive and detailed contract in seventeen numbered paragraphs covering eighteen folios of the printed record' which conferred upon Houghton Mifflin the exclusive volume rights to *Mein Kampf* throughout the United States ' "to publish and sell said work in editions, abridgments and selections" '. On balance it was felt that there was enough evidence to warrant the granting of a preliminary injunction:[9]

In a case such as this, where two editions of a book of great popular interest are being actively promoted in competition with each, it is obvious that much of the damage to a rightful owner of copyright, if any there be, will have been done by the time the action may be tried and final decree entered upon an accounting. Such owner needs protection now when the book is at the height of its sales, or else he may never be able to realize the fruits of ownership. Consequently it is settled in copyright cases that, if the plaintiff makes a prima facie showing of his right, a preliminary injunction should issue . . . In our view, on such of the facts as are not in dispute, the Plaintiff has so far established its right that it would be a denial of equity to allow the Defendants under the circumstances to sell their book with impunity until the final outcome of the action.

Clark's conclusion came out strongly against Stackpole.

Under the circumstances of entire absence of title or right in the Defendants, their claim that the equities are in their favor – that they are engaged in a service of great social value in thus publishing this book – seems indeed bold.

The decision, as handed down by the Circuit Court of Appeals, ruled that: 'The order is reversed and the cause remanded to the District Court with instructions to issue the preliminary injunction as prayed for.'

Now it was Stackpole's turn, but before they appealed the

case to the Supreme Court, two petitions were submitted to the Court of Appeals: one requesting a delay pending further clarification of the Court's ruling, the other requesting a 'rehearing' on the basis of new issues not dealt with previously by the Court. One of these had to do with the number of copies of *Mein Kampf* deposited with the Copyright Office in 1925–7. In order to bring suit, two copies of the work in dispute had to have been deposited, but Houghton Mifflin's Bill of Complaint before the District Court mentioned only *one* copy. Judge Clark's clerk, Elizabeth Horan, was not impressed with either of Stackpole's motions:[10]

The respondents [Stackpole] don't like your opinion very much! I think the theme of appellant, Houghton Mifflin, answers all the points raised about your opinion very well . . . It is true enough that granting the preliminary injunction right now is about like summary judgment against Stackpole. Withholding it would be the same thing against Houghton Mifflin. If the Court thinks its decision was right, and to my mind respondents have given us no reason to show us it isn't, it would be silly to nullify its effect by granting this motion [for delay].

Judge Clark was not inclined to change his mind either:[11]

Defendant [Stackpole] is certainly getting desperate and has turned up something of a technical point as to the deposit of copies. Yet this will not get it very far in the light of the recent decision of the Supreme Court in the *Washingtonian Publishing Co., Inc.* v. *Pearson et al.*, January 30, 1939, by McReynolds, J. (Black, Roberts, and Reed, JJ., dissenting), reversing App. D.C., 98 F. 2d 245. The Court held, analyzing all the various provisions of the copyright statutes, that deposit might be made at any time before action brought, and that after it had been made, damages might be awarded retrospectively before the deposit. Perhaps if it appears at the trial that the Plaintiff here has not made adequate deposit, it may have to withdraw the case and start over; but we certainly ought to do what we can to keep the Defendant tied up for the present. In the light of this decision, too, it seems perhaps reasonable to argue that all that is now required is that the Plaintiff shall have complied with the statute by the time action is brought, and that, since Hitler is admittedly a citizen of Germany, upon taking office in the winter of 1933, the admitted deposit of the one copy is now adequate under 17 U.S.C.A. section 12.

At any rate, it seems to me we ought to deny the petition for the rehearing. The point presented at this last desperate moment may properly be held too late for us to consider now, and we are justified in relying upon the allegations of Plaintiff's complaint in paragraphs 7 and 10, that the 'Proprietor complied in all respects with the' copyright act. Of course, this will not prevent the taking of testimony on the point when the trial on the merits comes on below . . . All the other points raised in this petition and the previous motion are but an attempt to retry matters we have passed upon.

Learned Hand's approach was similar to Clark's:[12]

If this is right, the objection comes down to this, that although the two deposits were not within the statute when made in 1925 and 1927, they were sufficient before the suit was brought. Surely we need not take away relief because a new copy was not deposited thereafter. It is a small hole but I can get my head and whiskers through. It is an absolutely new point too, not raised before. The rest of the petition is all old stuff.

Once the motions to delay and to rehear the case were turned down by the Circuit Court, Stackpole had no recourse other than to seek a writ of *certiorari* from the Supreme Court. The chief issue, according to Stackpole, was:[13]

For determination, for the first time in any Federal Court, including this Court, a construction of Section 8 of the Copyright Act in respect of the rights of non-resident aliens who are not citizens of any sovereign; that is to say who are 'stateless' . . . The Circuit Court of Appeals has spelled out that right from historical considerations of doubtful persuasiveness, and upon considerations of public policy which are reasonably subject for difference of opinion.

Should it be determined that stateless individuals could secure valid American copyrights, then the Supreme Court would have to address itself to section 12 of the Copyright Act of 1909 wherein was contained the requirement of depositing two copies of each new work, 'such compliance, of course, being a prerequisite to effective copyright registration and to the maintenance of copyright suit'. An ancillary question was whether the certificates secured from the Copyright Office upon the registration of a new work were *prima facie* evidence of the facts stated therein, as required by section 55 of the Copyright Act. As before, Stackpole insisted that 'in copyright cases title to a work must be alleged and shown in detail', and it was unreasonable to suppose that a registration certificate alone 'furnishes a sufficient basis for a preliminary injunction'.

Replying to Stackpole's petition, Houghton Mifflin dispensed with the issue of stateless individuals by taking refuge behind the Circuit Court of Appeal's ruling. Then they launched a frontal attack against Stackpole's other two points:[14]

The deposit requirements of Section 12 of the Copyright Act are not in controversy in this case; and the point urged by the defendants [Stackpole] not having been raised in the court of first instance [District Court] could not properly be raised for the first time in an appellate court.

Houghton Mifflin were especially annoyed at Stackpole's efforts to exploit a minor error in the original Bill of Complaint filed back in February 1939; almost a clerical mistake whereby only one copy had been deposited in 1925:

As the defendants [Stackpole] well know (although it does not appear in the present record), *two* copies of the volume with respect to which the author was described in the copyright application as a 'staatenlöser Deutscher' were deposited in the Copyright

Office with the copyright application. The reference in the Complaint to 'one' copy being deposited is incomplete and a motion has recently been made in the District Court to amend the Complaint in this respect, on which motion the defendants entered into a formal stipulation on file in the District Court that they will not allege surprise at the offer of proof that two copies of this volume were as a matter of fact deposited in the Copyright Office. If the Defendants wish to raise the point they could now do so in the District Court; they have not done so because they know that the facts would not support them . . . Whether Section 55 . . . dispenses with the necessity of all proof as to title of the proprietor to the copyright does not arise in this case, since the Court did not base its decision on this provision of the Copyright Act but rather held, as a matter of fact, that the proof was sufficient to establish, in the absence of contradiction, that the proprietor had had the right to apply for and obtain the copyright.

During the summer and early autumn of 1939, while awaiting the decision of the Supreme Court as to whether it would review the case, Stackpole were enjoined not to sell copies of their edition, but this did not deter other publishers. The Political Digest Press of New York City offered *Mein Kampf: An Unexpurgated Digest*, translated and annotated by B. D. Shaw. This was, more accurately, a pamphlet on cheap paper, thirty-one pages in length, containing sections on Propaganda, Democracy, and Race. At about the same time the Noram Publishing Company of Greenwich, Conn., put out *Mein Kampf (My Battle): A New Unexpurgated Translation Condensed with Critical Comments and Explanatory Notes* – a ten cent publication in thirty-two pages described by *Publishers' Weekly* as a 'tabloid, three columns to a page, on newsprint paper, with a lurid cover in red and black. It had a cartoon on the cover showing Hitler playing with a jigsaw map of Europe.' It was later estimated that the publisher sold half a million copies within the space of a few weeks.[15] Houghton Mifflin lost no time suppressing these editions, either by securing preliminary injunctions or by threatening to do so.

On 23 October 1939 the Supreme Court announced its decision to deny Stackpole's petition for a writ of *certiorari*.[16] As was customary, no explanation was given. One of the justices, Felix Frankfurter, absented himself from the deliberations, presumably on the grounds that he was known to be Jewish and a supporter of the Zionist cause.

It now seemed that Stackpole had finally exhausted all legal remedies, but Philip Wittenberg, the firm's attorney, offered one more avenue to explore. He was one of the leading authorities on copyright law, and saw a loophole here worth pursuing. In May 1940 he thus returned to the Second Circuit Court of Appeals, presided over this time by Learned Hand, with Harrie B. Chase and Robert P. Patterson as fellow jurists, and challenged the way in which the 1933 contract between Houghton Mifflin and Eher Verlag had been executed. In its Opinion rendered two months later, the Court concluded:[17]

If it were possible to try out the issue of the German publisher's title in an ordinary way, more could be said for a trial, but of course it is not. No further light can be thrown upon it, and we should be in precisely the same position after the trial as at present.

This is not true, however, of the execution of the assignment of July 29, 1933. We have passed upon its legal effect, and upon its validity in spite of the absence of the consular certificate required by Section 43 17 U.S. Code, but we did not finally pass upon its execution; that is to say upon the identity of the person who signed it and his authority to act for the German publisher. The fact that we held the *prima facie* proof of this sufficient for a temporary injunction is not conclusive. Ordinarily, it is true, the Plaintiff must establish his title without dispute, but we had to choose a denial of any real relief at all and accepting the case as made . . . Therefore, if the defendants [Stackpole] wish a trial upon the single issue of the execution of the assignment of Franz Eher

Nachfolger G.M.B.H. to the Plaintiff, they may have it. Judgment will be reversed so far; meanwhile the temporary injunction will remain in force.

Later in 1941 Eher Verlag received permission from Hitler to support Houghton Mifflin against Stackpole. A sworn statement was presented before an American consular official in Munich, verifying that the man who concluded the 1933 contract in the name of Eher Verlag had been duly empowered. Back went the case to the District Court, where, on 4 September, Houghton Mifflin were authorized to collect damages from Stackpole. A final figure of $15,250 was agreed upon and paid in full by the Telegraph Press on 25 October 1941.[18] This amount was based on the fewer than 12,000 copies that Stackpole were estimated to have sold. The records do not show whether any profits were ever turned over to refugee organizations, however. Furthermore, the Pennsylvania firm was not assessed for the more than $23,000 court costs incurred by Houghton Mifflin.

Although nothing had been specifically worked out with Eher Verlag, Houghton Mifflin felt justified in dividing legal costs equally with Hitler's publisher. Thus, before any royalties from the unabridged edition were paid to Curtis Brown for their client, Eher Verlag, half of the legal expenses were deducted. By this time it was December 1941. America was at war with both Japan and Germany, and Hitler was again and finally deprived of his American royalties.[19]

During the war Houghton Mifflin was not allowed to retain Hitler's royalties. Like other firms, it was subject to the provisions of the Trading with the Enemy Act, as well as a vesting order dated 28 August 1942, which required that all accumulated royalties and all future royalties had to be put into an account assigned to the Alien Property Custodian. After the war the United States Attorney-General succeeded the Alien Property Custodian, and became entitled to *Mein*

Hitler's *Mein Kampf* in Britain and America

Kampf's royalties. As of 31 March 1972, $92,616.59 in gross royalties had been paid to the United States Government, and the Attorney-General pays corporation tax on them to the Internal Revenue Service![20] Ironically, Stackpole's insistence that no royalties should go to Hitler was fulfilled after all.

Another irony was the way in which Reynal & Hitchcock's profits on *Mein Kampf* successfully assisted various refugee organizations. Quite early on, Alvin Johnson's Editorial Committee fastened upon one major group, the Children's Crusade, as beneficiary. It was the brainchild of Dorothy Canfield Fisher, who suggested that American children be weighed in school and then contribute pennies equal to their weight in pounds to aid refugee children. Prominent citizens were enlisted to support and plan the Crusade, and this was how Alvin Johnson learned of it and became a member of its board of directors. Dorothy Canfield Fisher and other writers composed plays and poems dramatizing the plight of refugee children, while the famous historian, Charles A. Beard, wrote an eloquent letter to the *New York Times* expressing his belief that children should have the experience of sacrificial giving. Some New York City debutantes put on a benefit fashion show featuring outfits that they had made themselves. About three weeks after the fund drive was over, Ms Fisher summed up the results:[21]

Several friends of the Children's Crusade for Children, interested in knowing a little more fully how the crusade's educational and relief campaign was carried on, have asked us to share this knowledge with your readers.

As is generally known, not one of the pennies collected from the school children of the United States during the Children's Crusade for Children has gone or will go for the cost of administering this nation-wide campaign. Every cent will go for the relief of war-stricken children. The active relief agencies to receive the relief funds will be determined by the jury of award when the collections are completed.

The campaign itself would not have been feasible if the money necessary for the conduct of the campaign had not been guaranteed in advance. This money has largely come from the publishers' profits on the unexpurgated American edition of Hitler's 'Mein Kampf', published by Reynal & Hitchcock. The trustees of this fund earmarked its contribution to the crusade specifically for administrative expenses. Therefore, any sums listed recently in public or official reports of expenditures made by the Children's Crusade have to do with the expenditures of these administrative funds, which until April 22 were the only funds received by crusade headquarters.

The total amount of the collections is not yet known, as it takes a long time to count pennies and nickels. It will probably not be very large as such things go, but quite large enough to do a great deal of material good. And there is no calculating the amount of moral good it will have done.

As the sky darkens tragically over our heads, in bitter violence and evil, it has occurred to many that this may be the last spontaneously undertaken, purely constructive effort of international good-will that we Americans may be privileged to make for a long time.

The administrative and promotional expenses for the Crusade came to about $35,000, which became the target for Alvin Johnson and the Reynal & Hitchcock Editorial Committee. A few days before the school fund drive took place, Curtice Hitchcock proposed contributing $50,000 from his own firm and from the Book of the Month Club. Much of this money had been held in trust pending possible damages from the Stackpole case, but it now seemed to Houghton Mifflin that the funds could be released in view of the prospect of not having to pay anything to Stackpole.[22] Thus, by the end of 1940 the Children's Crusade announced that it had collected about $140,000 over and above administrative costs, with the full amount to be divided among eight organizations concerned with helping refugee children.

One unresolved question still remains concerning *Houghton*

Mifflin v. *Stackpole*. When the judges of the Circuit Court made their decision in May 1939, were they influenced by other than purely legal considerations? Stackpole's attorney, Philip Wittenberg, was convinced subsequently that they were:[23]

When we got to the Circuit Court of Appeals, the judges there felt that in view of the strain, to say the least, and diplomatic relations with Hitler being as they were, the United States ought not to declare his copyrights invalid. I have seen a letter which one of them wrote to a friend of mine in which the judges expressed that opinion. There was nothing after that to be surprised about since we knew that there were grounds other than legal for the decision.

Those interested in the 'diplomatic' implications of the case were to be found of course in the Department of State, and therefore it comes as no surprise to learn that the Department took a lively interest in the case from the outset.

Almost a month before Houghton Mifflin sought their temporary injunction from the District Court, the firm's Vice-President, Ferris Greenslet, sent the following note to the State Department:[24]

Under the present condition of our relations with Germany, I think you may like to take a look at these enclosures, and pass them along to that division of the Department of State which considers matters of international copyright . . . It has seemed to us, considering the temperament of the author, that the expropriation of Hitler's private property, whether in direct violation of international copyright, or through a technical flaw in the specific protection, might give rise to an international incident.

Greenslet's letter, including its newspaper enclosures, was directed to the attention of Wallace McClure of the Treaty Division, who informed his departmental colleagues: 'Viewing the situation as a whole, it looks as though there may be a most unedifying legal battle between American publishers and also that there may be an international incident.'[25]

The State Department then asked Colonel C. L. Bouvé, Register of Copyrights, for his advice. He replied that if Houghton Mifflin's assignment from Hitler's publisher was in order, then 'that firm acquired thereby the exclusive right to translate the book' in America. However, if Hitler could be shown to be stateless at the time *Mein Kampf* originally came out, 'the question as to whether or not the German firm could acquire, through assignment of his literary rights in his work to it, the right to obtain a copyright may be debatable'.[26] In other words, if Hitler could not qualify for a valid American copyright, he probably could not assign that right to Eher Verlag. McClure again apprised his colleagues of the awkward situation:[27]

While the legal battle will probably commence between the American firm alleged to be violating the copyright and the American firm which claims to be the assignee of translating rights in this country, it seems evident that the facts are such as quite probably to bring about an international incident.

There is much reason to believe that the whole affair is extremely unfortunate from the point of view of this Government. The report regarding it from the Register of Copyrights, and still more the personal conversations which I have had with Col. Bouvé and with Mr. de Wolf, one of his assistants in the Copyright Office, indicates pretty clearly that the firm of Stackpole Sons proposes to commit an act which, in effect, will violate the rights of the man who is at the same time author of the book and Head of State in Germany.

It is a situation that is likely to bring trouble to the Government but which the Government seems to be altogether or almost powerless to do anything about in advance.

McClure also consulted the office of the Attorney-General, and followed the case closely once it came to court: 'In view of the importance of this case, it would seem appropriate that the Department keep in touch with it and for this purpose there is attached a letter asking the Clerk of the District Court for the Southern District of New York to transmit copies of the pleadings and other documents as they may accrue.'[28] Fortunately McClure's worst fears were not realized. The German government chose not to make an 'international incident' of it. As far as surviving records indicate, the State Department took no action, and only after the Circuit Court of Appeals rendered its decision on 9 June 1939 did McClure send out another office memorandum:[29]

This case, though involving on the surface only the national copyright law of the United States, may be accounted as of considerable significance from the point of view of international copyright relations . . . It is of more than passing interest that, in thus upholding Hitler's copyright, the Court paves the way to the maintenance of the rights of many victims of Hitler's measures.

Concurrently with his official involvement in the case, McClure also carried on a brief private correspondence with Judge Charles E. Clark of the Second Circuit Court of Appeals. McClure's letters and copies of Clark's replies have survived among the Clark papers, and there is no reason to believe that there are any serious gaps in the exchange. The first of McClure's letters was written on 13 June, the day after Clark's opinion was published in the newspapers. He began by reminding the judge of their meeting at a law symposium at the University of Tennessee in October 1938, and also congratulated him on his appointment to the Circuit Court of Appeals:[30]

As I have for some time handled the copyright work of the Department of State, and as I have also special personal interest in the matter, I am wondering if it would be within the bounds of convenience for the Clerk of the Court to send me a copy of your opinion, also, perhaps, copies of the pleadings in the case. If this is feasible, I assure you of my keen appreciation.

Clark replied the next day:[31]

In accordance with your letter of June 13, 1939, I am enclosing a copy of the opinion, as made by my secretary, in the case of Houghton v. Stackpole, involving the copyright of Hitler's 'Mein Kampf'. I will speak to the Clerk to see if copies of the pleadings are available.

I appreciate your kind note and recall with a great deal of pleasure our meeting at Knoxville last October and the enjoyable time we had there. I hope to see you again soon.

In a Postscript he enclosed the *Record on Appeal*. 'This is my own copy – will you please return it when you are through?' McClure retained the *Record on Appeal* for several weeks, shared it with the Register of Copyrights and the Legal Adviser's Office of the State Department, and then returned it.[32]

I cordially admire the neat way in which your decision, while according justice to the head of a great state, at the same time makes use of the occasion to assist the victims of some of the policies of his government. I am reminded of the way in which Marshall, by declaring [in *Marbury* v. *Madison*] a Federalist act, perpetuated one of the most vital Federalist policies.

Clark brought McClure up to date on Stackpole's efforts to secure a rehearing, the Court's denial of these motions, and Stackpole's intention to take the case to the Supreme Court. He also acquainted McClure with Stackpole's tactic of challenging Houghton Mifflin's compliance with section 12 of the Copyright Act concerning the deposit of two copies of a newly published work.[33]

Throughout the McClure–Clark correspondence, there is no hint of importunity, and it is worth noting again that all of the letters post-date the decision of the Circuit Court of Appeals. Thus, no overt pressure seems to have been exercised by the State Department, although it obviously took a keen interest in the case. Clark's law clerk, Elizabeth Horan, finds it inconceivable that the judges would have been swayed by any outside influence: 'I am quite sure that if any pressure were exerted for a particular decision, that it would have been fiercely resented and resisted by that Court – certainly by Charles Clark.'[31]

The possibility exists, of course, that someone from the executive branch of the government might have urged one or more of the judges to bear in mind the broader diplomatic and political implications of the case, yet there are no traces of this in their pre-conference Memoranda. There was evident sympathy among the judges for European refugee authors who might someday wish to have their works copyrighted in America. Both Clark and Learned Hand seemed to feel relieved that their preferences coincided with their sense of the law regarding this point, while at the same time they obviously suspected Stackpole of exploiting the situation for prestige and profit. Mrs Curtice Hitchcock summarized the feeling of many: 'Of course one of the things that delighted Reynal & Hitchcock about the final outcome was that copyright was assured to a number of refugees from Germany.'[35]

VII

Was there a third unabridged American translation of *Mein Kampf* in 1939?

When beginning research on the various English-language editions of *Mein Kampf* which appeared in the 1930s, we kept encountering allusions to one peculiar translation, the only known copy of which was in the Wiener Library of the Institute of Contemporary History in London. From its description by an interested scholar this text seemed to be one of three American translations published in the late 1930s:[1]

One, claiming to be 'the first and unexpurgated edition in the English language', had been printed late in 1938, by a German anti-nazi in the United States who revealed neither publisher nor place of publication. It is possible that even his name, Ludwig Lore, is fictitious. Hardly any reference has ever been made to this text.

More recently, in the latest English-language edition of Hitler's autobiography, the same conclusions are echoed:[2] 'The first was published in 1938 by an anti-Nazi German refugee in the United States, using the pseudonym, Ludwig Lore.' Another commentator, while accepting the identity of Ludwig Lore, nevertheless suggests that there are three identifiable American translations:[3]

One, entitled *Mein Kampf* (669 pp.), which was offered as 'the first complete and unexpurgated edition in the English language', was printed late in 1939 by Ludwig Lore, a German-born Social

Democrat, who up to 1942 was a columnist for the *New York Post*. Lore used the first German edition and wrote a militant introduction, but revealed neither publisher nor place of publication. Hardly any reference has ever been made to this text. More prominence was attained by two editions which appeared almost simultaneously in 1939, one, an unauthorized version (669 pp.), translated by a scholar whose identity the publishers, Stackpole and Sons, New York, refused to reveal; the other, (1,002 pp.) published in New York in collaboration with Reynal and Hitchcock by Houghton Mifflin and Co., the owners of the American copyright.

Even before we could scrutinize the Wiener Library copy in detail, we had a hunch that it must be the same as the Stackpole edition. It was too much of a coincidence that each had exactly 669 pages. A quick glance at the Library of Congress Catalogue confirmed this.

Mein Kampf: The first complete and unexpurgated edition published in the English Language (New York City, Stackpole Sons, 1939), pp. 669 . . . preface signed Ludwig Lore.

What has always thwarted the inquiries of scholars is the fact that there is no copy of the Stackpole edition in Britain, and no copy of the 'Lore' edition in America. The comparative rarity of the Stackpole edition is due to its having ceased publication within the space of a year, because it failed to defend its right to publication against the copyright holder, Houghton Mifflin. Besides, by 1939 the British issued their own unabridged version, published by Hurst & Blackett in conjunction with Hutchinson & Co. Ltd, and so there was no justification for importing copies from America.

Although it is impossible to juxtapose the two editions side by side, as the Wiener Library copy can only be seen in Britain, and the Stackpole copy only in America, one can at least compare sample photocopied pages. These establish that the two copies are identical. The preface by Ludwig Lore, the title page, the table of contents, and the pages of text are similarly numbered. In both editions every page contains the same number of words and each line corresponds perfectly with its counterpart in the other edition. What is more, the same typeface was used: namely, Janson Linotype; 12-point type on a 13-point slug. The mystery seemed to be solved: there had never been *three* American editions in 1939, only two – Stackpole's and the one authorized by Houghton Mifflin. The Wiener Library copy presumably was a stray Stackpole copy that found its way across the Atlantic.

Yet one thing continued to puzzle us. Why did it have no publisher's imprint? Would Stackpole have exported a certain number of copies after their edition had been suppressed in America? It certainly wouldn't have been the first time that a publisher had resorted to such subterfuge, yet this sort of activity was more typical of the nineteenth century when no Anglo-American copyright agreement existed, and non-copyrighted works flooded into both countries. Another possibility was that the title page of the Stackpole edition had been removed prior to its export abroad so that it would not immediately clash with the authorized British edition put out by Hurst & Blackett.

We tested this theory on Philip Wittenberg, the American lawyer who is an authority on copyright law, and who happened to be the attorney who represented Stackpole in 1939 in its litigation against Houghton Mifflin. To our great surprise he responded:[4]

With reference to some of the copies you may have seen, did you know that the Chinese on Formosa did a big copy job on this book, underselling the American edition? They used the Stackpole edition as the basis for their copying.

This revelation seemed the answer to all our questions, but how could we prove it? Where, in America, could we find an illegal reprint of the Stackpole edition, which was non-copyrighted and outlawed? Neither Houghton Mifflin, the current owners of the translation rights in America, nor the Stackpole Company, a subsidiary of the Commonwealth Communications Services, was able to assist us. Both were unaware that there had ever been such a reprint.

Being unable to compare the two editions directly was frustrating, but it occurred to us to experiment by making some obvious tests. Were the editions printed on the same stock of paper? If not, why not? Three different Stackpole copies consistently measured about 2·1 inches in thickness, excluding covers, when subjected to moderate pressure. A similar measure of the Wiener copy came out almost half as thick, or 1·2 inches. If Stackpole had had surplus copies on hand in 1939 and thereafter, it seems unlikely that they would have printed additional copies for export on light-weight paper. On the other hand, it was also hard to believe that the Taiwanese would have gone to such elaborate trouble to imitate that Stackpole edition. Not being sufficiently expert in such matters ourselves, we consulted two printers from what is perhaps the largest private printing company in the world: the R. R. Donnelley Company.[5] They discovered that in the Stackpole edition a printed line measured 25 picas, while the Wiener copy measured 26 picas. Similarly, the depth of the Stackpole page from the running head to the folio page number at the bottom was 4 points of a pica less than the Wiener copy. A comparison of the title pages and tables of contents showed that there were distinct differences in spacing between words. Slight variations in word spacing also helped to account for the differences in length of line throughout the text. At this stage it was clear that the Wiener Library copy was reset with similar type but on a different linotype machine; and if it were in fact a Taiwanese reprint, it was probably set from American type because this would have been the cheapest and easiest thing to do.

A third American translation of *Mein Kampf*?

Finally, what about Ludwig Lore, whose name appeared in the preface to the Stackpole edition? Here we are on firm ground. Lore's sons have preserved a letter from the publisher, enclosing a cheque for $75 in payment for the introductory pages.[6] Lore was born in Upper Silesia in 1875, became active in the Social Democratic Party, and emigrated to America in 1905. He soon found employment in New York with a German-American newspaper, the *New Yorker Volkszeitung*, and in 1919 became its editor-in-chief. As a Marxist of rather orthodox views, he was active in the early years of the American Communist Party, and in 1917 helped launch and edit *Class Struggle*, a twice-monthly magazine. After the war some states passed laws against certain activities of the Communist Party. Lore eventually gave himself up to the authorities and was found guilty and sent to prison under the provisions of the Illinois Sedition Act.

Upon his release he resumed his journalistic and political activities. A comparative moderate among radicals, he always sought to play the role of mediator among factions. Still an ardent Marxist, he was anti-Fascist in the 1920s and used his influence to expose the dangers of Nazism in the 1930s. As a freelance journalist he made frequent contributions to such major American magazines as *The Nation* and *New Republic*, and between 1934 and 1942 had a daily column in the *New York Post* entitled 'Behind the Cables'. Such a background in international relations and especially German-American affairs made it logical for Stackpole to commission him to write a preface for their new edition of *Mein Kampf*.[7]

In spite of this convincing array of evidence, the Wiener Library copy remains a mystery. We would feel more confident if we could locate another such facsimile, but inquiries to more than a dozen Taiwanese and Hong Kong libraries have yielded nothing. In fact, one of the latter explained why it was unlikely that such a Taiwanese reprint would be found: 'In general we try to avoid "pirate" editions for our own library stock, though occasionally some reach us as gifts.'[8] More puzzling is the Wiener Library accession number 1375 which suggests that the copy may have been acquired as early as 1946–7, although the detailed accession sheets have not survived. This is a good deal earlier than the dates that one generally associates with Taiwanese reprints. The volume could possibly have been printed in China prior to the revolution of 1949. However, the explanation which best fits the facts points to a Taiwanese reprint of what is undoubtedly the Stackpole edition.

Epilogue

Today there is only one English-language edition of *Mein Kampf* in print, translated by Ralph Manheim and published in the United States by Houghton Mifflin and in Great Britain by Hutchinson. Of the three unabridged versions appearing in 1939, Stackpole's was ruled illegal, while Reynal & Hitchcock's was allowed to go out of print in 1942 in favour of the new Manheim translation. Hutchinson might well have continued to reissue James Murphy's edition had the printing plates not been destroyed, ironically enough by German bombs.

Why Houghton Mifflin terminated their lease arrangement with Reynal & Hitchcock in 1942 is not altogether clear, owing to the disappearance of pertinent company files. At that time Manheim gained the impression that Reynal & Hitchcock's edition had not lived up to marketing expectations, but in fact by the beginning of 1942 more than 250,000 copies had been sold, due partly to a reduction in the selling price from $3.00 to $1.89. With sales figures like these, one might well conclude that rather than being discouraged by its performance, Houghton Mifflin were seeking to profit exclusively from the book.

As has been explained earlier,[1] Houghton Mifflin might have issued their own unabridged translation back in 1939 had it not been for Stackpole's challenge which forced them to rush into print with the Reynal & Hitchcock version. Thereafter Reynal & Hitchcock got most of the credit or

135

blame for providing American readers with *Mein Kampf*, no doubt to the moderate chagrin and regret of the true copyright owner, Houghton Mifflin. Moreover, the Reynal & Hitchcock edition with its elaborate notes and commentary was a bulky and expensive volume to produce, and so a new translation also meant that Houghton Mifflin would be able to reduce the size of the book by at least a quarter.

The quality of available translations was also a consideration. Murphy's version could not be sold in the United States due to existing Anglo-American marketing arrangements, and Stackpole's edition had been declared in violation of U.S. copyright laws; therefore only Reynal & Hitchcock's translation was readily accessible. Manheim recently recalled that the latter 'was done in a great hurry by no less than ten translators, some of whom I knew. I don't think that any of them had much of a command of both languages.'[2] Manheim may have confused Reynal & Hitchcock's translators with the ad hoc Editorial Committee selected solely for this project, but the point is well taken. That translation had the virtues as well as the shortcomings of a group effort which suffered from pressures of time and competition. As for Manheim, Houghton Mifflin knew the quality of his work because in early 1942 he was putting the finishing touches to a translation of Konrad Heiden's *Der Führer* for them.

Negotiating the new translation was Robert N. Linscott, and it is evident from his letter to Manheim in February 1942 that he anticipated an early publication date: 'I am delighted to know that you will translate at the rate of $6 a thousand [words], plus $250 for notes and index . . . And I am particularly glad that you can begin work in a few days and complete it by the first of July.'[3] Linscott was overly sanguine about the book's completion, however. It did not appear until the autumn of 1943, but it has remained in print ever since.

Manheim had some distinct notions on how Hitler's prose should be rendered. In his Translator's Note he observed:[4]

Epilogue

Most of Hitler's stylistic peculiarities represent no problems for the translator. The mixed metaphors are just as mixed in one language as in the other. A lapse of grammatical logic can occur in any language. An English-language Hitler might be just as redundant as the German one; a half-educated writer, without clear ideas, generally feels that to say a thing only once is rather slight.

There are, however, certain traits of Hitler's style that are particularly German and do present a problem in translation. Chief among these are the length of the sentences, the substantives, and the German particles.

A translation must not necessarily be good English, but it must be English such as some sort of English author – in this case, let us say, a poor one – might write. On the other hand, it would be wrong to make Hitler an English-speaking rabble-rouser, because his very style is necessarily German.

No non-German would write such labyrinthine sentences. The translator's task – often a feat of tightrope-walking – is to render the ponderousness and even convey a German flavor, without writing German-American. In general I have cut down the sentences only when the length made them unintelligible in English.

Recently Manheim commented: 'The gimmick to my translation of *Mein Kampf* is that I tried at least to render some of the oddities of Hitler's style.'[5]

In the years immediately following the Second World War Americans could readily purchase Manheim's translation, while British readers had either to rely on second-hand copies of Murphy or to import the American edition. In Germany there was a total ban on *Mein Kampf*.[6] As executor of all surviving Nazi property, the Bavarian state government sought to prohibit the sale of the book throughout the world. Initially this suppression was consistent with the Allied de-Nazification policy, and the Federal Republic later agreed that it was contrary to national self-interest to sanction the publication of so hateful and incriminating a work. It was felt that there was enough anti-German feeling remaining

137

from the war without awakening old memories and reopening wounds.

Others both in and out of Germany took the position that the evil of Nazism could only be exorcized by facing and scrutinizing it. Each new generation must understand how and why Hitler came to power and to what extent the people and conditions in Germany had contributed to his rise. For this purpose *Mein Kampf* was regarded as one of the essential documents of the inter-war decades, sometimes not appreciated at the time, but remarkably revealing in retrospect.

By the 1960s it was apparent to the British copyright holder of *Mein Kampf*, the Hutchinson Publishing Group Ltd, that popular as well as academic interest in Nazism continued. Hutchinson's chairman, Sir Robert Lusty, therefore urged his firm to reissue a British edition of Hitler's autobiography. To this end he secured permission from Houghton Mifflin to utilize Ralph Manheim's translation. The volume was to be published in the autumn of 1965, but quite unexpectedly Sir Robert ran into stiff opposition. As he later recorded in his memoirs:[7] 'Almost simultaneously I found we were under attack from what I would have thought to be two altogether disparate bodies – the West German Government . . . and the Board of Deputies of British Jews.' He could understand the fury of the Jews because of 'their relentless persecution under Nazi Germany.' He knew that there were a number of people in Hutchinson itself who bitterly opposed the reissue, but he was totally unprepared for his board of directors to cancel the project while he was on an extended summer holiday abroad. When he learned that this had been done his first inclination was to resign, but eventually he was persuaded to stay on but to postpone publication indefinitely. Several years passed before he revived his plans. Again he encountered opposition from many quarters, but this time he pushed ahead nevertheless, and in 1969 presided over the publication of a hard-cover edition. The selling price was set intentionally high so as to avoid any imputation of catering to a mass audience. Three years later a paperbound version was roundly condemned as a betrayal of earlier promises not to seek a wide distribution for the infamous volume, but Sir Robert claimed that a soft-cover book selling for £1.95 was in no sense a cheap popular paperback.[8]

During the 1960s Hutchinson found it far easier to refute West German objections than to deal with Jewish protests. Regarding the first, Hutchinson pointed out that the Nazis had never repudiated their contract with Hurst & Blackett, and therefore, as the successors to that company, they possessed a valid copyright for the British and Commonwealth market. When it came to Jewish opposition there was no legal point at issue, rather a moral one. Most British Jews could not help feeling that ready access to *Mein Kampf* would only promote anti-semitism and play into the hands of post-war Fascist organizations. The way that the Federal Republic of Germany failed to prosecute known Nazis after the war reinforced their conviction that sympathy for Nazism still prevailed and that making this book available again lent some shred of respectability to Hitler. Thus, while they bitterly resented Hutchinson's decision, they admitted ambivalence. On the one hand they did not want to remind people of what Hitler stood for, and yet, on the other, they did not want people to forget. Deep and honest disagreements persisted. Most Jewish organizations were critical of Hutchinson while the Council of Christians and Jews came out in support of publication.

In their Publisher's Note Hutchinson attempted to justify their point of view:

The German authorities and some sections of the Jewish community continue to object to the circulation of this book in any form, thinking that it may prove damaging to new understandings and friendships. These doubts we can understand but cannot share.

Hitler's *Mein Kampf* in Britain and America

The origin of Hitler is almost irrelevant. What is important is that he existed, that he brought tragedy to his people and the world, and that there are still sympathisers in many parts of the world today. *Mein Kampf* is a compendium of their prejudices and ignorance, whether they belong to the German, British or any other nation.

It is necessary therefore that Hitler, their prototype, 'the master of the inept, the undigested, the half-baked and the untrue', should be understood. *Mein Kampf* is an introduction to his mind and methods, and as such should be readily available for study by all and, in our view, in every language.

Perhaps when it comes to understanding the origins and devastating course of National Socialism the familiar observation of George Santayana says it best: 'Those who cannot remember the past are condemned to repeat it.'

Notes

I. *Mein Kampf* in Britain, 1930–39

1. For the various editions and estimated sales figures of *Mein Kampf*, both in German and in translation, see: O. J. Hale, 'Adolf Hitler: Tax Payer', *American Historical Review*, LX (July 1955), 830 42; C. Caspar (pseud.), '*Mein Kampf*: A Best Seller', *Jewish Social Studies*, XX (Jan. 1958), 3–16; 'The Story of *Mein Kampf*', *Wiener Library Bulletin*, VI (Dec. 1952), 31–2. For background information on Hitler's publisher, Eher Verlag, see: O. J. Hale, *The Captive Press in the Third Reich* (Princeton, 1964), pp. 15–26. Prof. D. C. Watt's introduction to the most recent English edition of *Mein Kampf*, published by Hutchinson Publishing Group Ltd, is also valuable.

2. See below, Chapters IV–VI concerning the American editions of *Mein Kampf*.

3. We have endeavoured to mention all of these individuals in the acknowledgments at the beginning of this volume.

4. Our thanks to Mrs G. M. Dugdale for permission to quote the letter in her possession. The letter is marked only 'Sunday', but from internal evidence can be dated as 21 Sept. 1930. Sir John Wheeler-Bennett informs us that the allusion to Jack W. B. refers to him, and that Hugh Latimer was at that time editor of the *Bulletin of International News*.

5. Basic biographical information for E. T. S. Dugdale (1876–1964) may be found in *Burke's Peerage, Baronetage and Knightage*. Concerning Blanche Elizabeth Campbell Balfour (1880–1948), a biographical entry is to be found in *Who Was Who, 1941–1950*. In 1936 she published a two-volume biography of her uncle,

Notes

Arthur James Balfour. In 1973 an edition of her diary, entitled *Baffy*, was compiled by N. A. Rose.

6. The contract was typical of its kind. Eher Verlag retained the copyright and disposed of the translation rights. The royalty would vary from 10% to 20% depending upon how many of the initial 5,000 copies were sold at 18s. each.

7. The most important references to Thost at the Public Record Office are in: F.O. 395/468 (1932), ff. 132–41; F.O. 371/18868 (1935), C. 7381, ff. 290–1. See also: *Hansard's Parliamentary Debates* (11 May 1933), cols. 10, 55–6. Thost later wrote a book about his observations of England: *Als National Sozialist in England* (München, 1939). Thost's role in the negotiations for the abridgment of *Mein Kampf* was described by Cherry Kearton.

8. The extracts appeared in *The Times*: 24 July 1933, pp. 13–14; 25 July, pp. 15–16; 27 July, pp. 13–14; 28 July, pp. 15–16.

9. *Observer*, 15 Oct. 1933, p. 5.

10. *Spectator*, 20 Oct. 1933, pp. 530–1; *The Times*, 13 Oct. 1933, p. 20; *New York Times*, 18 Oct. 1936, pp. 1–3 of magazine supplement.

11. *The Times*, 13 Oct. 1933, p. 20; *New York Times*, 15 Oct. 1933, p. 1. The former American Ambassador to Germany was James W. Gerard.

12. Copies of C. Weizmann to G. Dawson, 27 July 1933, and of L. Stein to C. Weizmann, 25 July 1933, enclosed in C. Weizmann to R. Vansittart, 27 July 1933; Public Record Office, F.O. 371/16759, C. 6871, ff. 2–7.

13. E. T. S. Dugdale, 'National Socialism in Germany', *English Review*, LIII (Oct. 1931), 565–73. We are greatly indebted to Mrs G. M. Dugdale for drawing our attention to this article.

14. See Chapter III below concerning the unexpurgated London edition of 1939.

15. Although most of the records of Eher Verlag were destroyed at the end of the war, there are very useful remnants on microcopy T-580, roll 832. These were kindly brought to our attention by the staff of the Captured Records Branch, Military Archives Division, of the National Archives in Washington. Where data are missing, we have been able to approximate the figures, whether it be the amount of British tax withheld, the net royalties in pounds sterling, or their equivalent in German marks.

16. At the end of 1933 this left only 1,275 copies on hand from the 2nd to 8th editions, each impression being about 1,750.

17. The basis on which the advance on royalties was paid for 1933–4 is unclear, due to the disappearance of the records. Because tax had already been paid on the advance of £350, no tax was withheld during 1934 and part of 1935. During the 1930s, British tax on royalties tended to be about 25%. For the British home market, royalties on the popular edition were figured at 10% of the retail price, while copies exported to the colonies yielded a somewhat lower return.

18. In compiling the list of reviews, we were greatly assisted by a memo from Hurst & Blackett to Eher Verlag, 25 March 1936, Library of Congress, Division of Manuscripts, Rehse Collection, MS box 437.

II. The British Foreign Office and *Mein Kampf*

1. Rumbold to Simon, 26 Apr. 1933, Dispatch No. 36, in E. L. Woodward and R. Butler (eds.), *Documents on British Foreign Policy*, Second Series, Vol. v (London, 1956), pp. 47–55.

2. Weizmann to Dawson, 27 July 1933, with enclosures: F.O. 371/16759, C. 6871, ff. 2–7.

3. F.O. 371/18880, C. 5596, ff. 303–9; F.O. 371/19899, C. 2579, no pagination.

4. Rennie Smith, *Autobiography* (typescript presumably written in the 1960s): Bodleian Library, MSS Eng. Hist., D296–7. The quotation comes from ff. 309–10. Duchess of Atholl, *Working Partnership* (London, 1958), pp. 200–1.

5. Gaselee to Atholl, 5 Dec. 1935, F.O. 371/19938, C. 159, f. 132.

6. Atholl to Gaselee, 7 Jan. 1936, *ibid.*, f. 131.

7. Gaselee to Atholl, 8 Jan. 1936, *ibid.*, f. 133.

8. *ibid.*, f. 130.

9. F.O. 370/478, L. 7880, ff. 168–78: Gaselee to Gage, 13 Dec. 1935; Gage to Gaselee, 25 Mar. 1936; and Sargent to Gaselee, 17 Apr. 1936.

Notes

10. Sargent to Phipps, 2 Apr. 1936, F.O. 371/19899, C. 2579, no pagination.

11. Phipps to Sargent, 7 Apr. 1936, F.O. 371/19938, C. 2920, ff. 136–8.

12. Kirkpatrick to Wigram, 27 Apr. 1936, F.O. 371/19938, C. 3492, f. 144.

13. F.O. 371/19938, C. 3455, no pagination.

14. *ibid.*

15. Earl of Avon, *The Eden Memoirs: Facing the Dictators* (London, 1962), p. 374.

16. Letter of Viscountess Waverley to J. J. Barnes, 13 June 1973.

17. F. O. 371/19938, C. 3455, no pagination.

18. Among the Atholl papers at Blair Castle are a number of letters relating to the Friends of Europe Pamphlet no. 38. See especially: Laurie to Atholl, 22 Aug. 1936; Atholl to Smith, 25 Aug., 27 Aug., 4 Sept., and 14 Sept. 1936; Smith to Atholl, 16 and 23 Sept.; Wigram to Atholl, 12 and 25 Sept.; Atholl to Robertson, 31 Aug.; and Atholl to Pares, 27 Aug., 1936.

19. Woodward to Wigram, 21 June 1936, F.O. 371/19938, C. 5510, no pagination. Wigram's Minute is dated 23 June 1936. *ibid.* Eden's Minute is dated 19 July 1936.

20. Ogilvie-Forbes to Viscount Halifax, 6 Dec. 1938, in Woodward and Butler (eds.), *Documents*, Third Series, Vol. III (London, 1950), pp. 386–8.

21. D. Dilks (ed.), *The Diaries of Sir Alexander Cadogan, 1938–1945* (New York, 1972), p. 139.

22. *Forum*, CI (May 1939), 268.

23. J. W. Wheeler-Bennett, *Munich: Prologue to Tragedy* (New York, 1948), p. 163.

24. A. L. Rowse, *Appeasement: A Study in Political Decline, 1933–1939* (New York, 1961), p. 117.

25. I. MacLeod, *Neville Chamberlain* (London, 1961), p. 210.

26. Rowse, *Appeasement*, p. 38.

27. C. Thorne, *The Approach of War, 1938–1939* (London, 1968), pp. 11–13.

28. K. Feiling, *The Life of Neville Chamberlain* (London, 1946), p. 328.

29. Letter of D. N. Dilks to J. J. Barnes, 8 Feb. 1977.

30. D. C. Watt, *Personalities and Policies* (Notre Dame, 1965), pp. 118–19.
31. R. Vansittart, *Lessons of My Life* (New York, 1943), p. 148.
32. The Houghton Mifflin edition of the Dugdale translation, entitled *My Battle*, was given to Roosevelt by the firm in October 1933. This copy is in the Roosevelt Library, Hyde Park.
33. As quoted in Thorne, *Approach of War*, p. 13.

III. James Murphy and the 1939 London edition

1. Two competing and unabridged editions of *Mein Kampf* appeared in New York at the end of February 1939. One was published by Reynal & Hitchcock under a license agreement from Houghton Mifflin; the other edition by Stackpole Sons. For further details about these two American editions, see below, Chapters IV–VI.
2. W. Strang to Maj. F. L. Fraser, 9 Feb. 1939, F.O. 371/23005, C. 1677, ff. 26–7. Ensor's review appeared in the *Spectator*, 24 March 1939, pp. 491–2.
3. 'The Story of *Mein Kampf*', *Wiener Library Bulletin*, VI (1952), 31.
4. In addition to the cordial assistance of Mrs Murphy, the others who have aided us are gratefully included in the Acknowledgments at the beginning of this volume.
5. It is our hope eventually to collaborate with Mrs Murphy on a biography of her late husband.
6. Dieckhoff to the German Foreign Ministry, 29 March 1938, in the possession of the Auswärtiges Amt in Bonn. Hereafter this source will be cited as A.A. Bonn.
7. Propaganda Ministry to Foreign Ministry, 29 June 1937. A.A. Bonn.
8. Frau Dr Greta Lorcke Kuckoff was one of the few members of the Rote Kapelle not to be executed. Her memoirs, *Vom Rosenkranz zur Roten Kapelle*, were published in East Berlin in 1973. She has been most gracious in responding to our letters of inquiry.
9. From a brief typescript account (1973) of her husband's life by Mrs Mary Murphy; hereinafter referred to as '1973 account'.

Notes

10. This and other quotations come from Mrs Murphy's '1973 account' and from her diary entries.

11. Eher Verlag to Hurst & Blackett, 21 Nov. 1938. Captured German Records, microcopy T–580, roll 832.

12. *The Bookseller*, 30 Dec. 1938, p. 1424; *Daily Telegraph*, 31 Dec. 1938, p. 11.

13. W. T. Kimber to J. Murphy, 4 Jan. 1939, in the possession of Mrs Murphy.

14. Eher Verlag to Pownschab, 9 Jan. 1939; and memo of telephone conversation between Foreign Ministry and Reichskanzlei, 4 Feb. 1939; A.A. Bonn.

15. 'The Nazi Propaganda Machine', an address to the Royal Institute of International Affairs, 16 Sept. 1941, copy in the possession of Mrs Murphy.

16. *The Bookseller*, 23 Mar. 1939, p. 445; and '1973 account'.

17. *The Times*, 24 Mar. 1939, p. 20; *Spectator*, 24 Mar. 1939, p. 492; and *Daily Telegraph*, 23 Mar. 1939, p. 16. For other reviews of Murphy's translation, see: *Observer*, 26 Mar. 1939; *The Times Literary Supplement*, 25 Mar. 1939; and *Evening News*, 23 Mar. 1939.

18. A. Hitler, *Mein Kampf* (New York: Reynal & Hitchcock, 1939) and *Mein Kampf* (Boston: Houghton Mifflin, 1943). For a discussion of the Reynal & Hitchcock translators, see Chapter IV. For further details concerning Ralph Manheim, the translator of the Houghton Mifflin edition, see the Epilogue.

19. In a 1941 retrospective fragment, Mrs Murphy recalled the details concerning royalty payments to her husband. Also in her possession is a letter of 15 Aug. 1939 from their literary agent.

20. The memorandum of K. Pownschab bears the date of 12 Apr. 1939. See also: Pownschab to H. Dieckhoff, 19 Apr. 1939. Both are in A.A. Bonn.

21. *Sunday Times*, 8 Aug. 1965, p. 7.

22. Eher Verlag to Hurst & Blackett, 5 May 1939; Hurst & Blackett to Eher Verlag, 12 May 1939; and Curtis Brown to Eher Verlag, 23 May 1939; Captured German Records, microcopy T–580, roll 832.

23. For coverage of the illegal French edition, see: *The Times*, 6 Mar. 1934, p. 13; 5 June 1934, p. 14; and 21 June 1934, p. 13.

Notes

IV. The American reaction to *Mein Kampf* 1933–39

1. The contract of 29 July is reprinted on pp. 10–15 of the *Record on Appeal, United States Circuit Court of Appeals for the Second Circuit, Houghton Mifflin Company, Plaintiff–Appellant, against Stackpole Sons Inc., and the Telegraph Press, Defendants–Respondents.* Hereafter this source will be cited as *Record on Appeal*.

2. *New York Times*, 18 Aug. 1933, p. 16.

3. *ibid.*, 21 Sept. 1933, p. 17.

4. *ibid.*

5. *Annual Report* for 1934, pp. 49–50.

6. Conn to Roosevelt, 31 Aug. 1933, National Archives, Dept of State Decimal File H-D 811.918/257.

7. M. E. Osherman to Roosevelt, 6 Sept. 1933, National Archives, Dept of State Decimal File H-Th 811.918/258.

8. On 28 Sept. 1933 Moffat wrote identical replies to Conn and Osherman. They are attached to the incoming letters.

9. Scaife to Roosevelt, 13 Oct. 1933, Roosevelt Library, Hyde Park. Houghton has preserved many such letters of protest as alluded to by Scaife.

10. *New York Times*, 11 Oct. 1933, p. 21.

11. *ibid.*, 15 Oct. 1933, p. 1.

12. The list of reviews was enclosed in a letter from Houghton Mifflin to Eher Verlag, 8 Apr. 1936, Library of Congress, Manuscript Division, Rehse Collection, MS box 437.

13. *Kansas City Star*, 14 Oct. 1933. The article was also preserved by the Press Section of the Auswärtiges Amt in Bonn.

14. The sales figures in this chapter are based on Captured German Records, microcopy T-580, roll 832. In some instances the files are incomplete and therefore approximations have been made. The value of the Reichsmark fluctuated during the 1930s, but for the sake of convenience and uniformity we have taken 2.6 Reichsmarks as equal to one dollar. Both at that time and later, sales figures were mentioned in the press and elsewhere, but these were generally based on a calendar year, whereas Houghton Mifflin accounted to Eher Verlag biannually, on 31 March and 30 September.

15. In 1936 the corporation income tax was increased from 13.75% to 15%, but in order not to complicate the picture for the decade unduly, we have used the larger percentage throughout.

16. German Consulate, Boston, to Embassy, Washington, 19 Feb. 1937, A.A.Bonn, files 32/4 and 32/13.

17. Kent to Teele, 4 March 1937, *ibid.*

18. Consulate, Boston, to Embassy, Washington, 4 Mar. 1937; Embassy, Washington, to Foreign Ministry, Berlin, 8 Mar. 1937, *ibid.* The Lloyd George article appeared in the 22 Sept. 1936 issue of the *Herald Tribune*, p. 7.

19. Unidentified newspaper cutting included among the materials on Captured German Records, microcopy T–580, roll 832.

20. Reynal & Hitchcock to Federal Trade Commission, 16 Mar. 1939, in the possession of Harcourt Brace Jovanovich.

21. Letter of Mrs Curtice Hitchcock to J. J. Barnes, 14 Jan. 1977.

22. Letter of Graham Hutton to J. J. Barnes, 11 Mar. 1973.

23. *Mein Kampf* (New York: Reynal & Hitchcock, 1939), p. ix.

24. Hutton to J. J. Barnes, *op. cit.*

25. Letter of W. L. Langer to J. J. Barnes, 19 Mar. 1973. Prof. Langer played more of a significant role than he recalls, but not in behalf of the Editorial Committee. He served as Houghton Mifflin's chief scholarly adviser, reinforcing their wish to tone down Shuster's Introduction and notes. See for example: H. A. Laughlin to C. Hitchcock, 14 Jan. 1939; Laughlin to F. Greenslet, 23 Jan. 1939; Laughlin to Greenslet, 2 Feb. 1939; in the possession of Houghton Mifflin Co.

26. Letters of G. N. Shuster to J. J. Barnes, 22 Mar. 1973 and 12 Dec. 1976.

27. Affidavit of Edward J. Stackpole, Jr, 17 Feb. 1939, *Record on Appeal*, pp. 46–51.

28. Letters from Soskin and from Reynal & Hitchcock were reprinted in *Publishers' Weekly*, cxxxv (7 Jan. 1939), 32–5.

29. Affidavit of E. J. Stackpole, *op. cit.*

30. A copy of the contract between Reynal & Hitchcock and Houghton Mifflin Company, dated 18 Feb. 1939, is to be found in the possession of Harcourt Brace Jovanovich. The chief reason why Houghton Mifflin delayed signing the agreement with Reynal & Hitchcock was because the Boston firm hoped that Eher Verlag

Notes

would be forthcoming with active legal and financial support. See Laughlin to Hitchcock, 9 Jan. 1939, in the possession of Houghton Mifflin Co.

31. Letters of Shuster to J. J. Barnes, *op. cit.* For further details about Houghton Mifflin's misgivings about the Introduction and notes, see note 25 above.

32. In December 1938, Houghton Mifflin asked the literary agency of Curtis Brown in New York to notify Eher Verlag that Stackpole and possibly other American publishers were prepared to reprint *Mein Kampf.* In a cable from the Munich firm to Curtis Brown, dated 19 Dec. 1938, it was pointed out: 'As you know, we have made an agreement for America with Houghton Mifflin and in virtue of this contract there exists no possibility of transferring the right to any other publishing firm.' That, however, was not really the point at issue, and Eher Verlag were reminded that Houghton Mifflin wished to lease the rights for the full text to Reynal & Hitchcock, while at the same time preventing Stackpole from issuing an unabridged version. In response, Eher Verlag to Curtis Brown on 1 Feb. 1939: 'In reply to yours of January 12, we have not now under consideration the publishing of an enlarged version of MEIN KAMPF. Should it be decided at a later time to proceed with an English translation, we would naturally get into com-munication with Houghton Mifflin.' This was essentially the same response which Eher Verlag had made to Hurst & Blackett in November 1938, and it was similarly ignored in the face of moving events. The above extracts were quoted in a letter from Laughlin to A. Dawson, 19 July 1940, in the possession of Houghton Mifflin Co.

V. The Stackpole challenge

1. *United States Circuit Court of Appeals for the Second Circuit: Houghton Mifflin Co. Plaintiff–Appellant, against Stackpole Sons Inc., and the Telegraph Press, Defendants–Respondents*, p. 41. Hereinafter referred to as *Record on Appeal*.
2. *ibid.*, p. 44.
3. Letters of Virginia Soskin Reis to J. J. Barnes, 10 Jan. and 27 Apr. 1977.

149

Notes

4. Letter of G. W. Stewart to J. J. Barnes, 6 Dec. 1976.
5. *Record on Appeal*, pp. 47–51.
6. *Publishers' Weekly*, CXXXI (30 Jan. 1937), 467.
7. Reis to Barnes, *op. cit.*
8. *ibid.*
9. Letter of P. Wittenberg to J. J. Barnes, 7 May 1973. Wittenberg was a leading authority on the law of copyright and author of: *The Protection and Marketing of Literary Property* (New York, 1937).
10. Letters of J. B. Mussey to J. J. Barnes, 22 Nov. and 14 Dec. 1976.
11. A brief sketch of Mussey's career and his translation of *Mein Kampf* appeared in the *Saturday Evening Post*, CCXIX (9 Nov. 1946), 4.
12. Mussey to Barnes, *op. cit.*
13. Reis to Barnes, *op. cit.*
14. Mussey to Barnes, *op. cit.*
15. A copy of this statement was enclosed in a letter from Soskin to Ludwig Lore, 17 Apr. 1939, in the possession of the Lore family.
16. *Publishers' Weekly*, CXXXV (18 Mar. 1939), 1129.
17. Reis to Barnes, *op. cit.*
18. Mussey to Barnes, *op. cit.*
19. *Publishers' Weekly*, CXXXV (7 Jan. 1939), 32.
20. Mussey to Barnes, *op. cit.*
21. Wittenberg to Barnes, *op. cit.*
22. Letter of Mrs Curtice Hitchcock to J. J. Barnes, 27 Jan. 1977.
23. *ibid.*
24. *Record on Appeal*, p. 23.
25. Reis to Barnes, *op. cit.*
26. *Record on Appeal*, p. 51.
27. The memorandum of 17 Feb. 1939 is in the possession of Harcourt Brace Jovanovich.
28. Soskin to Old Corner Bookstore, 2 Feb. 1939; *Record on Appeal*, p. 28. According to Curtice Hitchcock, Soskin was a personal friend of Brentano's manager, and therefore received special consideration. With the exception of Brentano's and Marshall Fields of Chicago, which displayed both editions, most stores in major cities favoured the Reynal & Hitchcock edition in terms of space and promotion. See Hitchcock to F. Greenslet, 25 Feb.

Notes

1939; and E. Reynal to Greenslet, 17 Mar. 1939; in the possession of Houghton Mifflin Co.

29. *ibid.*, p. 26.

30. Letter of C. Hitchcock to Houghton Mifflin, 18 Feb. 1939, in the possession of Harcourt Brace Jovanovich.

31. *Record on Appeal*, p. 131.

32. D. C. Watt, 'Die Bayerischen Bemühungen um Ausweisung Hitlers 1924', *Vierteljahrshefte für Zeitgeschichte*, VI (July 1958), 270–80.

33. Letter of C. Hitchcock to F. Greenslet, 3 Mar. 1939, in the possession of Harcourt Brace Jovanovich. By June 1939, Reynal & Hitchcock estimated that they had sold about 45,000 copies of *Mein Kampf*. See Hitchcock to Greenslet, 7 June 1939, in the possession of Houghton Mifflin Co.

34. Letter of M. Wood to C. Hitchcock, 27 Mar. 1939, in the possession of Harcourt Brace Jovanovich.

35. Letter of Wood to Hitchcock, 7 June 1939, in the possession of Harcourt Brace Jovanovich.

36. During the course of February 1939, Reynal & Hitchcock pleaded with Houghton Mifflin to withhold all royalties to Hitler pending the settlement of the case. Once the District Court declined to grant a temporary injunction on 28 February, Houghton Mifflin acquiesced, and thereafter it was much easier for Reynal & Hitchcock to undermine Stackpole's publicity campaign. See Hitchcock to Greenslet, 22 and 25 Feb. 1939, in the possession of Houghton Mifflin Co.

VI. *Houghton Mifflin* v. *Stackpole* on appeal

1. *Brief on Behalf of Houghton Mifflin Company, Plaintiff–Appellant* (11 Apr. 1939), pp. 4–6; copy in the possession of Harcourt Brace Jovanovich.

2. *Brief on Behalf of Stackpole Sons Inc., and the Telegraph Press, Defendants–Respondents* (20 Apr. 1939), p. 8; copy in possession of Harcourt Brace Jovanovich.

3. *ibid.*, p. 25.

4. *ibid.*, p. 28.

Notes

5. E. R. Horan's comments of 23 May 1939 are to be found in Box 9 of the case files of the C. E. Clark papers, Yale Law School Library.

6. Clark's pre-conference Memorandum of 24 May 1939 is in the C. E. Clark papers, Yale Law School Library, as well as in the L. Hand papers, Harvard Law School.

7. L. Hand's pre-conference Memorandum of 23 May 1939 may be found both in the Clark papers and the Hand papers, *op. cit.*

8. A. N. Hand's pre-conference Memorandum of 24 May 1939 may be found in both the Clark and the L. Hand papers, *op. cit.*

9. *Federal Reporter*, CIV (St Paul, 1939), 306–12.

10. Comments of E. R. Horan, 21 June 1939, *op. cit.*

11. Pre-conference Memorandum of C. E. Clark, 23 June 1939, *op. cit.*

12. Pre-conference Memorandum of L. Hand, 26 June 1939, *op. cit.*

13. *Petition for Writ of Certiorari* . . . (1939), no. 375. Copy in the possession of Harcourt Brace Jovanovich.

14. *Brief for the Respondent in Opposition to Petition for Writ of Certiorari* (1939), in the possession of Harcourt Brace Jovanovich.

15. *Publishers' Weekly*, CXXXVI (22 July 1939), 228. In 1974 Senator Alan Cranston said he was the one who provided notes for the tabloid edition and that it sold with incredible rapidity. See J. Toland, *Adolf Hitler* (New York, 1975), paperback edition, p. 724.

16. *Supreme Court Reporter*, LX (St Paul, 1940), 131.

17. *Federal Reporter*, CXIII (St Paul, 1940), 627–8; No. 341.

18. A photostatic copy of the cheque is in the possession of Harcourt Brace Jovanovich.

19. Intra-office Memorandum of 6 November 1942, in the possession of Houghton Mifflin Co. Until the outbreak of war in December 1941, Hitler received royalties from the abridged 1933 edition and subsequent re-issues. He also received half of the $5,000 advance which Reynal & Hitchcock paid Houghton Mifflin upon publication of the unabridged edition.

20. Letter of Irving Jaffe, Deputy Assistant Attorney-General, Civil Division, Department of Justice, to J. J. Barnes, 13 Dec. 1972.

21. Letter of D. C. Fisher to the editor, 22 May 1940, *New York*

Notes

Times, 24 May 1940, p. 18. For other references to the Children's Crusade in 1940, see: 26 Feb., p. 17; 10 Mar., section 2, p. 1; 16 Apr., p. 21; 21 Apr., section 4, p. 8; 25 Apr., p. 7; 29 Apr., p. 13; 24 May, p. 42; 31 Aug., p. 5; and 25 Dec., p. 14.

22. Letter of C. Hitchcock to H. A. Laughlin, 16 April 1940, and Laughlin to Hitchcock, 18 April 1940; in the possession of Harcourt Brace Jovanovich.

23. Letter of P. Wittenberg to J. J. Barnes, 7 May 1973.

24. Letter of F. Greenslet to S. Welles, 3 Jan. 1939, National Archives, Department of State Decimal file 811.544 Mein Kampf–3 US–Y.

25. McClure memo of 4 Jan. 1939, Decimal file 811.544 Mein Kampf–1 US KFC.

26. Letter of C. L. Bouvé to R. W. Moore, 14 Jan. 1939, Decimal file 811.544 Mein Kampf–5 US/LW.

27. McClure memo of 23 Jan. 1939, Decimal file 811.544 Mein Kampf–6 USV.

28. McClure memo of 6 Feb. 1939, Decimal file 811.544 Mein Kampf–7 US/KFO.

29. McClure memo of 16 June 1939, Decimal file 811.544 Mein Kampf–8 US/LW.

30. McClure to Clark, 13 June 1939, C. E. Clark papers, Yale Law School Library, Box 23, general correspondence.

31. Clark to McClure, 14 June 1939, *ibid.*

32. McClure to Clark, n.d. [28 June 1939], *ibid.*

33. Clark to McClure, 29 June 1939. The last letter in this series is dated 1 July 1939 and is from McClure to Clark, thanking him for further explaining the case, *ibid.*

34. Letter of E. R. Horan to J. J. Barnes, 27 June 1976.

35. Letter of Mrs C. Hitchcock to Barnes, 14 Jan. 1977.

VII. A third American translation of *Mein Kampf*?

1. 'The Story of *Mein Kampf*', *Wiener Library Bulletin*, VI (Dec 1952), 31.

2. A. Hitler, *Mein Kampf: With an Introduction by D. C. Watt* (London, 1969), pp. xv–xvi.

Notes

3. C. Caspar (pseud.), '*Mein Kampf*: A Best Seller', *Jewish Social Studies*, xx (Jan. 1958), 10.

4. P. Wittenberg, *The Protection and Marketing of Literary Property* (New York, 1937). Letter from P. Wittenberg to J. J. Barnes, 26 Nov. 1973.

5. Messrs James A. Garard and Price Plank of the R. R. Donnelley Co. in Crawfordsville, Indiana, kindly assisted me with identifying and comparing typefaces.

6. William Soskin of Stackpole Sons to Ludwig Lore, 17 Apr. 1939; in the possession of Kurt and Eugene Lore.

7. The best obituary notice for Lore is in the *New York Times* (9 July 1942), p. 21. See also: *Wilson Library Bulletin*, xvii (Sept. 1942), 8. In connection with the abridged edition of *Mein Kampf* (Boston, 1933), Lore wrote a valuable review for the *Nation*, cxxxvii (1 Nov. 1933), 515–16. Standard reference works to periodicals, such as *The Reader's Guide*, cite a number of his articles for the 1930s. The best source for his involvement in the early years of the American Communist Party is: T. Draper, *The Roots of American Communism* (New York, 1957), pp. 76, 86–7, 132, 203–4. For background on the laws against Communists and the arrests of the early 1920s, see: R. K. Murray, *Red Scare* (Minneapolis, 1955).

8. Letter from University of Hong Kong Library to J. J. Barnes, 28 June 1978.

Epilogue

1. See Chapter iv.

2. Letter of R. Manheim to J. J. Barnes, 28 Oct. 1978.

3. Linscott to Manheim, 3 Feb. 1942, in the possession of Houghton Mifflin Co.

4. A. Hitler, *Mein Kampf* (Boston, 1943), p. xiii.

5. Manheim to Barnes, 28 Oct. 1978.

6. This ban persisted until 1979 when a German court of appeals ruled that literature from the Nazi era could henceforth be bought and sold.

7. Sir Robert Lusty, *Bound to be Read* (London, 1975), pp. 203–10. This chapter was also reprinted in *The Bookseller* (13 Sept. 1975), pp. 1646–8.

8. *ibid.*

Index

155

Index

Index

157

Index

22643384R00112

Made in the USA
Middletown, DE
05 August 2015